MEET THE GIRL TALK CHARACTERS

Sabrina Wells is petite, with curly auburn hair, sparkling hazel eyes, and a bubbly personality. Sabrina loves magazines, shopping, sleepovers, and most of all, she loves talking to her best friends.

Katie Campbell is a straight-A student and super athlete. With her blond hair, blue eyes, and matching clothes, she's everyone's idea of little miss perfect. But Katie has a few surprises for everyone, including herself!

Randy Zak has just moved to Acorn Falls from New York City, and is she ever cool! With her radical spiked haircut and her hip New York clothes, Randy teaches everyone just how much fun it is to be different.

Allison Cloud is a Native American Indian. Allison's super smart and really beautiful. But she has one major problem: She's thirteen years old, five foot seven, and still growing!

Here's what they're talking about in
Girl Talk

SABRINA: Katie, he called! He actually called!

KATIE: Who called?

SABRINA: Raymond Foy! The TV producer, silly!

KATIE: Seriously? What did he say?

SABRINA: We did it! We're on "Hitline U.S.A"! We're taping in Minneapolis on Saturday. We'd better get working on our costumes and everything.

KATIE: Wow! That's great! Stacy is going to be pretty mad when she hears about this.

SABRINA: I know, and I hope I'm there when she finds out so I can see her face!

STAR QUALITY

By L. E. Blair

GIRL TALK® series created by Western Publishing Company, Inc.

Produced by Angel Entertainment, Inc.

Western Publishing Company, Inc., Racine, Wisconsin 53404

 Library of Congress Catalog Card Number: 91-070575 ISBN: 0-307-22017-6   A MCMXCI

Text by Leah Jerome

Chapter One

"Hurry up, you guys! It's coming on," I cried, running into the living room. I didn't even turn around to see if my friends were following me. I looked at my watch — 7:29 — only one minute to go until our favorite show, "Hitline U.S.A.," came on the air.

On the show, people come out in costumes and lip-synch to their favorite songs. The best group wins $5,000. The host, Rick Stevens, is incredibly, totally gorgeous. My best friends, Katie Campbell, Randy Zak, and Allison Cloud, and I try to watch it together every Saturday night. We take turns going to each other's house. Tonight we were at my house.

"Don't worry, Sabs," Randy said, carrying a bowl of popcorn into the room. "We've got a whole minute left."

"So, Sabrina, do you think you can keep our bet?" Katie asked, following Randy into the room and putting four glasses down on the coffee table.

I glanced at Katie and Randy with a smile on my face. "Sure! I just know I can sit still this time."

See, there's something about the music on "Hitline U.S.A." that just gets me going, and before I know it I'm up dancing around the room. Katie, Randy, and Al decided to make a bet that I couldn't sit through a show without jumping up and dancing.

"And here's your host, Riiiick Stevens!" the announcer suddenly called out.

"Shh!" I said, plopping down on the floor. "It's on!" We crowded around the TV. Rick Stevens ran out on stage with a major smile. His shoulder-length blond hair looked great — as usual.

"Do you think he was born with that tan?" Randy asked, pulling off her black cowboy boots. "I mean, he's that dark all year long." She sat down Indian-style on the couch.

"Maybe he goes to a tanning salon," Katie replied, sitting down next to Randy. Katie didn't take her shoes off, though. The laces of her white tennis shoes stayed tied, just like the ribbon in her long blond hair. Katie is one of the neatest people I know. I think she got it from her mother.

Randy kicks her shoes off whenever she gets a chance. She says that shoes restrict her. I never thought about it like that until I met Randy. Randy is what my mother calls a free spirit. I think she's really cool. Moving to Acorn Falls from New York City at the beginning of the school year was a big change for her. She says there's so much more going on all the time in New York. I believe it. I'd love to go to New York. But I think Randy's really starting to like it here. She'll never change her New York style, though.

"Well, he does live in Los Angeles," Allison added, gracefully lowering herself to the floor next to me. Al is the most graceful person I know. She's tall and thin and she moves like a ballet dancer. She's also incredibly gorgeous. With her long, thick black hair and exotic Native American looks, Al definitely stands out in a crowd. She was even offered a modeling contract with *Belle* magazine once.

"I don't care how tan he is," I said. "He looks great. Look at that awesome outfit." Rick was wearing black pleated pants, a white mock turtleneck, and a teal-and-black-checked blazer. I sighed. "He's practically to die for."

"Come on, Sabs," Randy said, throwing a pillow at me. "He's pretty cute, but I wouldn't *die* for him."

"Who's the celebrity panelist this week?" Katie asked curiously. "Hitline U.S.A." has a panel of four people that judge the acts. Three of the panelists are on every week but the fourth one is always a surprise celebrity from music, television, sports, or the movies. Last week it was a famous soap opera star.

Rick Stevens began to introduce the panelists. The regulars are pretty boring. I mean, they're on every week. Then the camera focused on the celebrity of the week.

"Psych!" Randy yelled. "It's Stacy Q., my favorite drummer!"

"Wow!" I gasped. I don't know as much about music as Randy does, but I do know that Stacy Q. is the best female drummer on the charts. She just started working on a solo career. I also know that she started out playing for a high school band in her hometown, just like Randy plays for Iron Wombat. I know all of this because I read about her in one of the magazines I subscribe to. Randy says I have more subscriptions than a dentist's office, but I think it's the best way to pick up tips for my acting career.

"Stacy Q. is totally the most," Randy continued. "I saw her in concert once back in New York — she was unbelievable. She's got the best touch."

"Hey, they're starting," Katie said, pointing to the television.

The first group came out on stage. There were five people all dressed as mummies. The sixth person was wearing a red leather suit. They started lip-synching to Michael Jackson's song "Thriller." They were pretty good.

"Their costumes were kind of cool," Katie said after they finished.

"Isn't that song a little old, though?" Allison asked. "I mean I like oldies, but. . ."

"It's old news," Randy agreed. "It was definitely way before our time."

"And that guy's lip-synching wasn't so hot," I added, having watched the act very critically. If I'm going to be an actress, I know I have to have a critical eye. There was an article last month in my favorite magazine, *Young*

Chic, about Price Richards, one of my favorite actors. Price said that when he was studying acting, he always watched everything with a critical eye. Then he would go home and write a review about the movie, or play, or whatever. When he acted in plays and movies himself, he tried to keep in mind what he had learned from writing his reviews. I thought it sounded like a great idea, so I've been trying to develop my critical eye since then.

The panelists agreed with us about the first act. Scores are based on three categories — originality, presentation, and lip-synching. You can win up to ten points in each category from the panelists for a total of thirty points. Rick Stevens read the scores. "For originality, a four. For presentation, a nine. And for lip-synching, a six. That gives you a score of nineteen! Nice job!" Then a commercial came on.

"I would love to be on 'Hitline U.S.A.,'" I said with a sigh. "It would be so much fun. Just think of the national exposure I'd get. Maybe an agent would recognize my talent and sign me to a contract, and take me to New York. . ."

"Snap out of it, Sabs," Randy said, snapping her fingers. She grinned at me. "You'll have your whole life planned in a minute."

I giggled. Planning my whole life? Right. I'm lucky if I can pick out what I'm going to wear tomorrow. I'm the impulsive type. Maybe it's because I'm a Pisces. Pisceans go off in a lot of different directions all the time.

"What's up, kids?" Sam asked, walking into the room. Sam is my twin brother. Everyone always says that we look a lot alike but I don't really see it. I mean, we both have red hair and freckles, but other than that we're completely different. Sometimes Sam likes to say that we can't really be twins because he was born four minutes earlier than I was. Please. Four minutes is nothing. I know he just wants to remind me that he's older than I am. But I'm definitely more mature.

"Dude!" Randy said, holding up her hand. Sam walked over and slapped it with his.

"What are you guys doing?" Nick asked, following Sam into the room. Jason was right behind him. I think boys always travel in packs. I never see my brother going anywhere alone.

"We're watching 'Hitline U.S.A.,'" I said. "So, you guys had better pipe down."

"What?" Sam asked in mock shock. "You think we're noisy? I am so insulted."

"Dudes, I'm starving!" Nick exclaimed, sitting down next to me on the floor. He turned his blue eyes to me. "Are you hungry, Sabs?"

"I could eat," I admitted. Katie, Randy, Al, and I had gone to Fitzie's, the place to hang out after school, and had ice cream sodas. But that was hours ago.

"Let's order some pizza," Jason suggested. "How much money do you dudes have?"

I rolled my eyes and looked over at Sam. I don't know what he does with his allowance, but he's always running out of money. And then who do you think he borrows from? Me. I guess he thinks that's what sisters, and twins, are for. We share practically everything, anyway.

Sam dug deep in his jeans pockets and found two lint balls, a stubby pencil, an old fuzzy piece of gum, a rubber ball that our dog, Cinnamon, had obviously been chewing on, a pocketknife, and fifty-four cents. Typical, I thought. And he makes fun of the mess in my purse.

"Sabs?" Sam asked with a pleading kind of

tone.

I tried to look stern, as if I were going to give him a lecture about budgeting his money or something. But I couldn't. I had to admit he looked kind of cute like that, even if he was my brother.

"No problem," I said, handing him four dollars. "If we all chip in two dollars, we'll have plenty."

"Thanks for covering me," Sam said to me, squeezing onto the couch next to Randy and Katie. "So, who's ordering?"

"You're a dog!" Jason exclaimed with a smile.

"And you're weak!" Sam replied, grinning back.

Boys can be so incredibly weird. They insult each other all the time, but they act as if they're complimenting each other or something. I just can't figure them out — and I've got four brothers. You'd think I'd know. My mother and I talk about this a lot. She says they're a mystery to her, too.

"Well, Jason, you get to call for it," Nick added. "That's what you get for being tame!"

Jason threw a pillow at Nick. "Well, what do

we want on it?"

Suddenly, the commercial ended.

"Hey, you guys, it's back on!" I exclaimed, bouncing up and down a little. "Tone it down!" My eyes were glued to the screen, but I knew Jason was standing there waiting for an answer. "Jason, just don't get anchovies, okay?"

"Cool," he said and ran into the kitchen. He was back before the next act came on. "The pies will be here in twenty minutes."

"Shh!" Sam said.

There were three women in the next group. They were wearing really funky, Day-Glo clothes. They lip-synched to "Hold Off" by In Touch.

"This tune rocks," Randy said, pulling her drumsticks out of her back pocket and beating a rhythm on the edge of the coffee table.

"I love the way they're dancing," I said. "That's a cool step." I jumped up and started swinging my arms back and forth like the group was doing. Then they did this little hopping-type skip and spun around. Really cool.

I was in the middle of twirling around when I saw Katie, Allison, and Randy staring at me. I was about to say something when I remembered the bet. Uh-oh!

"The next pizza we have is on you, Sabs!" Katie exclaimed, laughing. I stopped twirling and plopped down on the floor. I hate to lose bets.

"Whoa! What a performance!" Rick exclaimed after the lip-synching group had finished. "For originality, a perfect ten. For presentation, another ten. And for lip-synching, yet another ten. That gives you a perfect score of thirty. Congratulations!"

"Cool," Randy said, nodding. "They really deserve to win."

"I'll bet nobody else even comes close," Katie agreed.

Katie was right. The next three groups were nowhere near as good. The show ended and the girl group that sang "Hold Off" won the $5,000.

"Hey, check it out!" Nick shouted, just as Allison was about to turn off the television. "'Hitline U.S.A.' is coming to a city near you for auditions!"

"Wouldn't it be great if they came near here," I said wistfully. "I know we could make it on the show if we put an act together."

"You know they won't come to Acorn Falls," Randy said. "It's probably just a gimmick or something. Besides, I'm sure you have to know someone to get on that show."

Randy was probably right. She knows a lot about television because her father is "in the business." He directs music videos and commercials.

"You guys would be great, though," Nick said, grinning at me. Katie is always saying that Nick has this major crush on me. I don't buy it. I mean, he went out with Stacy the Great Hansen all last year in sixth grade. Stacy thinks she's a gift to all boys or something. And she still considers Nick her personal private property, even if they have "broken up." Anyway, Nick is great, not to mention really cute. But he's my brother's best friend, and all the magazines I read always talk about the trouble involved in going out with your brother's friends.

"Yeah," Sam agreed. He pulled the rubber ball out of his pocket and tossed it to Cinnamon, who started chewing on it. "I could see you on that show, Sabs."

"Thanks," I said, a little surprised. Not that

Sam doesn't support me. He does — but usually not to my face. He always sticks up for me and stuff, but he almost never compliments me.

"You're such a ham!" he continued, grinning at me.

"Very funny," I shot back. "Actresses have to be."

"That's probably true," Jason said. "You can't just be yourself."

"And Sabs is a really good actress," Nick continued. "I mean, she stole the whole show as Frenchie in *Grease*."

I have to admit I was pretty good in *Grease*. I played Frenchie in the junior high school production of *Grease*, and everybody told me that I stole the show. I mean, Stacy Hansen was the star because she played Sandy but I got the most applause — and the most laughs. I guess I'm destined to be a comic actress. Someone told me I've got great timing, whatever that is.

The pizza finally came, and we all dug in. After we demolished both pies, the guys went outside to play some hoops in the driveway, and my friends and I ran upstairs to my bedroom. The best thing about being the only girl in the family is that I get my own room. And my room is very cool. It's on the third floor, in the attic. The roof is slanted in all these directions, and I've got a bunch of skylights, too. My room is unique.

"Sabs, do you actually read all of these magazines from cover to cover?" Randy asked, going through my stack of old ones in the corner.

"Of course I do," I answered. "You never know what you might learn from these magazines. Besides, you know you like to take those quizzes and stuff, too."

Randy snorted. "That one we took last week was totally bogus," she said. "'How Flirtatious Are You?' just didn't do it for me."

"But you were just as interested in your score as we were," Katie replied, grinning. She walked over to the mirror and picked up my hairbrush. As she brushed her long blond hair, Katie looked over at me and winked. We had read this article two weeks ago about brushing your hair often to get the follicles moving around a lot. It supposedly helps your circulation and stimulates hair growth or something. I don't know if it works, but I do know that we had all started carrying hairbrushes with us.

14

Even Randy — and her hair is spiked on top!

"Hey, do you think Arizonna looks like Rick Stevens?" I asked, plopping down on my bed. Arizonna was a new kid in school. He had just moved to Acorn Falls from California. I'd love to go to California. That's where Hollywood is. Anyway, he's got longish blond hair, just like Rick Stevens has. And he's really cute, too.

"Kind of," Randy replied, flipping through last month's issue of *Belle*. "I mean, if you squint your eyes and tilt your head a little."

I giggled. "You're too much, Ran," I said, tossing a stuffed animal at her.

"So, Sabs, when are you going to ask him out?" Katie asked. I blushed and played with the neon friendship bracelets on my wrist that Arizonna had given me. I did have kind of a crush on him, but it wasn't a big deal.

"I'm not going to ask him out!" I answered. "We're just good friends."

Allison, Randy, and Katie all looked at each other and raised their eyebrows.

"What?" I asked in mock surprise.

"Nothing," they all replied at once.

I leaned back against my pillows and stared at the new poster of Alek Carreon that I had hung on my ceiling. He was beautiful. And he was a great actor, too. I wondered what it would be like to act in a movie with him.

"Hey, let's take this quiz," Katie said a few minutes later, interrupting my daydream. "It's called 'Find Your Career.'"

Randy groaned but put down her magazine and came over to sit next to me on the bed.

"*A stewardess!*" Al exclaimed after we finished taking the quiz. "I'm supposed to be a stewardess?" She looked kind of dazed.

Randy laughed. "At least, you're not going to be fire fighter like I am," she said.

"I just can't picture that," Katie replied. "No way."

"Well, I can't see Sabs in the army either," Randy added, looking at me.

Giggling, I stood up and started marching around the room, saluting everyone. "I'd be a great soldier," I said, sitting down again. "Besides, khaki and olive green are big colors this year. At least I'd be fashionable if nothing else."

Everyone laughed.

"I can't see you with a crew cut though," Katie said. "It's just not you."

Sighing, I pulled a handful of my thick, curly auburn hair in front of my face and acted as if I were really disappointed. "I guess you're right. I should stick to acting."

"Good idea," Randy said. "Listen, I'm still hungry. Is there any ice cream in the house?"

"Hey, you're at the Wellses'," I said, standing up and putting my hands on my hips. "Of course we have ice cream."

"Let's go chow!" Randy exclaimed, and we all followed her down the stairs.

That night, I fell asleep thinking about what Nick had said. And I dreamed that I won first place on "Hitline U.S.A." and Rick Stevens gave me a check for $5,000. I could just hear him say, "And here is our most talented winner in TV history . . . Sabrina Wells!" When I walked forward I was wearing an army uniform, right down to the combat boots. Then I took off my hat and I had a crew cut! Sometimes I have the weirdest dreams.

Chapter Two

"We're going to start reading *Romeo and Juliet* today," Ms. Staats said the next day in English class.

"Psych!" I whispered to Randy, who sits behind me. I love reading plays out loud in English. It's good training. And Shakespeare is a classic. I mean, his plays are great! When I'm a famous star, I'm going to go to England and act in all his plays.

"I hope she picks you to read," Katie said softly. Katie does not particularly like to read out loud in class. Actually, neither does Al. Al read last week, though, so she was off the hook today.

"Sabrina, why don't you be Juliet today?" Ms. Staats asked, pushing her black cat's-eye glasses up on her nose. Ms. Staats is my favorite teacher. She's so incredibly cool! She doesn't talk down to us as other teachers do and she treats us like adults, kind of — I like that.

I cleared my throat. I wondered who was going to be Romeo. Not that it really mattered. I mean, this was only an English class. It wasn't as if it were a real play or anything. But still.

"And, Arizonna, you can be our Romeo today," Ms. Staats continued.

"Just friends, huh?" Randy asked in a whisper, leaning forward on her desk.

I felt my body blush coming on. My whole body got really warm and I knew I was turning bright red. Then I giggled. Arizonna, even though he's really cute and everything, is not my idea of a Romeo. He's a surfer dude and says "awesome" and "most excellent" all the time. Definitely not tall, dark, and handsome material.

"Certainly," I replied in a fake haughty tone.

So then we started reading about the Montagues and the Capulets. I have to admit, I got really into it. I forgot that the rest of the class was sitting there, and I just got caught up in the story. It was so incredibly sad!

When the bell rang at the end of class, I

almost jumped in my seat. I had just about forgotten that I was in school.

"Thanks very much to all the people who read today, especially Sabrina and Arizonna," Ms. Staats said, holding up her hands as if to keep all of us in our seats.

"Hey, this Shakespeare dude is most excellent!" Arizonna burst out. Everyone laughed.

"I'm glad you enjoyed it," Ms. Staats replied, grinning at us. It's so funny to see a teacher grin. I mean, they smile every once in a while — well, some of them do — but I've never seen any of my other teachers grin!

"Okay, I'd like all of you to read Act III for tomorrow," she continued. "See you then."

The rest of the day flew by. I thought in Shakespeare's language for a few more classes before I was normal again. I think that's a good sign, though. I was reading that the really good actresses get totally into their roles. I was totally into Juliet. I think I must have still been in the role at lunch, because I couldn't stop thinking how cute Arizonna was.

"Hi, guys. Anybody else want ice cream?" I asked as I reached Al's locker after the last class of the day. "I've been craving a super-deluxe sundae since sixth period."

"I'm up for it," Randy said. "Let's hit Fitzie's."

When we walked into Fitzie's, there was a huge crowd looking at something on the wall in the back. "I wonder what's going on?" Allison said.

"Well, there's only one way to find out," I replied and worked my way through the crowd. There are a lot of advantages to being short — getting through crowds is one of them.

"Ohmygosh!" I screamed over my shoulder to my friends as I read the poster on the wall. 'Hitline U.S.A.' is coming to Acorn Falls! See, you guys didn't believe me. I told you the show would come here."

I stood on my tiptoes to try to see where my friends were. They were still at the back, but I could see Allison's head above the crowd. "Katie!" I yelled loudly. "Write this down. Next Saturday at Patterson High School. One P.M. to four P.M. Individual or group auditions to get on a special youth episode of 'Hitline U.S.A.' No costumes needed for the audition. The five best lip-synching groups will be selected to compete on the show."

After I finished reading, I pushed my way back through the crowd. "Did you get all that?" I asked Katie.

"Got it, Sabs," she replied. I glanced at her notebook to make sure she had gotten everything.

"See, I'm going to be discovered," I said, teasing my friends as we walked back to an empty booth.

"Why do I get the feeling we're about to get involved in something?" Randy asked.

"What do you mean?" I asked innocently. They didn't really think I was going to be a lip-synching group of one, did they?

"I have the same feeling," Katie said, smiling at me. "We're about to make our lip-synching debut."

We all laughed. My friends knew me really well.

"But, Sabs," Katie continued. "Don't get your hopes up. I mean, there're probably going to be hundreds of kids trying out."

"I know," I said. Katie is very logical. She's got her feet planted firmly on the ground and works hard to bring me back down to earth. I think we balance each other out. I mean, it's good to get your hopes up once in a while. But she was right. There were probably a lot of kids who were just as excited as I was.

"But we have as good a chance of getting on the show as anyone else," I continued. "Someone's got to be on the show, right?"

Katie agreed to that. She couldn't really disagree. It was a logical argument, if I do say so myself.

"What song are we going to do?" Allison asked. "And we're going to have to practice, right?"

"Oh, no," a loud voice came from behind me. "Don't tell me that you girls actually think you could get on 'Hitline U.S.A.'"

I turned around and saw Stacy Hansen walking toward us. Her friends, Eva Malone, Laurel Spencer, and B. Z. Lattimer, were with her, of course. "Don't you know that you have to have talent and good looks to be on TV?" she said with a perfect little flip of her long honey-blond hair.

"Oh, then I guess you don't even have to bother trying out," Randy said. We all giggled. Our group doesn't really get along with Stacy's group, and we don't exactly hide it. I think

Stacy gets upset because we just don't worship her like she thinks we should.

"Very funny, Rowena," Stacy replied, trying to get Randy mad by calling her by her real name. Randy hates the name Rowena. "But not only are we going to try out, we are going to win. We'll get on that show and win first prize. And when Rick Stevens sees me, he'll want me on the show every week."

"Right," I said, trying to keep calm. But Stacy really knows how to push my buttons. I was getting pretty worked up. "Oh, yeah? We could win if the audition was tomorrow."

"Dream on, Sabrina," Eva said. "On the night of the show, you'll be sitting at home watching us on TV." Stacy and her friends all laughed.

"Well, it would be kind of fun to watch you humiliate yourselves on national TV," Randy said with a grin. "We might even have to tape that."

"Come on, girls," Stacy said to her friends. "We don't need to listen to this. They're just jealous." She turned around and walked right into Arizonna.

"Hey, Stace, where's the fire?" Arizonna

asked, as he caught her arm.

"Oh, hi, Arizonna," Stacy said in a sickeningly sweet voice. It was enough to give me cavities. In fact, my teeth hurt. Stacy has had a major crush on Arizonna since he moved here. I looked at my friends and winked. I love to watch Stacy in action. She's a definite wealth of material — stuff I can use in acting. "We were just telling Sabrina and her friends that we're auditioning for 'Hitline U.S.A.' Now we're off to work on our act."

"Most cool," Arizonna said, pushing me over and squeezing into our booth next to me. "You babes should most definitely audition, too."

Stacy looked a little like a fish, the way her mouth keep opening and closing and no sound came out. I couldn't help it, I laughed. Stacy glared at me. Then she turned on her heel and marched right out of Fitzie's. Her friends hurried after her. I looked at Al, Katie, and Randy, and we all cracked up. There's nothing quite so satisfying as getting Stacy really worked up.

"Dude, it's a definite possibility," Randy said to Arizonna after we had gotten ourselves under control. Arizonna, of course, had no idea what we were laughing about. For some reason, most of the guys at Bradley Junior High just can't see what a phony Stacy is. I don't understand it. They think she's kind of cute and everything. As Randy would say, go figure.

"I guess it does sound like fun," Katie added.

"Katie, your enthusiasm is bowling me over," I joked. Katie giggled.

"Maybe you should try out, too, Zone," Randy said.

"Like, it's not my scene," Arizonna replied, snitching a spoonful of my super-deluxe sundae. "Do you babes know what you're synching to, yet?"

We all shook our heads. I had a feeling it might take us a while to pick out a song. I mean, we all have very different tastes and everything. When we go to the video store to pick out movies, it can take us hours. I like teen adventure-type movies, Randy loves horror, and Al is into these strange intellectual foreign movies. Luckily, Katie will watch just about anything. She says none of them are real anyway. So I wasn't really sure how we were all going to pick out a song.

"Maybe I can, like, give you a hand," Arizonna suggested.

"Do you mean you want to pick out our song?" I asked, confused.

"No, I thought I'd be kind of like a director," Arizonna replied with a flip of his longish blond hair. His hair flip was definitely more attractive than Stacy's. "It would be most excellent to be behind the scenes."

"You mean you would tell us how the act is and what we're doing wrong and stuff?" I asked.

"Is that cool?" he asked, standing up.

"That would be awesome," Randy replied. "What do you girls say?"

"Sounds good," Katie said as she took a sip of her chocolate malted milk shake. "We could probably use the help."

"It's a good idea," Al added.

"Coolness," Arizonna said. "I've got to jam. I'll catch ya'."

"Bye, Arizonna!" I called after him. "So, when are we going to start practicing?" I asked my friends. "We don't have much time."

"Why don't we meet tonight, after dinner?"

Katie asked. "It'll be okay with my mom — as long as I get my homework done first."

"I have to check with my parents first," Allison replied. "But I'm sure it will be okay."

"How about at my place?" Randy suggested. "Less distractions." Randy lives alone with her mother in this converted barn. It's really wild. She doesn't have any brothers or sisters or anybody running around. It's a good place for us to concentrate. And being an actress requires total concentration.

"I'd better motor," Randy said, jumping out of her seat.

"Why doth thou rush?" I asked in my best Elizabethan English — just like Shakespeare would have written.

"Because if I'm late getting started on my homework I'll never make it to your house tonight," Randy said to me. "Catch you after dinner — unless you're going to be hanging out on some balcony with Arizonna, your Romeo."

Chapter Three

"Sabs!" Randy exclaimed when she answered the door a few hours later. "Check this out!"

I walked into the living room area. Katie and Al were already sitting on the couches. "Is that a video camera?" I asked, looking at a camera on a tripod.

"Yup," Randy said, grinning at me. "D just sent it to me from New York. I found it waiting for me when I got home."

Randy calls her father D and her mother M. I guess it's a New York thing. Randy's mother won't let us call her Mrs. Zak, either. She's always telling us to call her by her first name, Olivia. I think Al and Katie have a hard time with that sometimes, because they're always forgetting. I kind of like it, though. Olivia's really cool. She's an artist, and she even does shows in Minneapolis. Anyway, I think Randy inherited a lot of her mom's artistic talent. Lately, she's really gotten into photography. She takes her camera everywhere, and she's always shooting pictures of Al, Katie, and me. I have to admit that I really like posing for her, too. It's a great way to get a portfolio started. A portfolio is a collection of photographs of oneself, and every actress needs one.

Randy was saying just last week that she wanted to try a video camera. I guess she must have mentioned it to her father and he sent her this video camera. It was probably easy for him to get her the camera, since he is a director and all.

"That's like total fate!" I said. "Now we can tape ourselves and see how we look. See, we were meant to do this audition."

"All we need now is a song," Katie pointed out.

"And we've got a lot of practicing to do, too," Allison added.

"Details, details," I said with a wave of my hand. I knew we'd come up with something. I had this feeling now that we were going to be discovered. I can't explain it. But I just knew. Besides, my horoscope for the last few days had mentioned that something big was in my immediate future. This was definitely it.

"Well, what song are we going to do?" Randy asked, plopping down on the couch.

"Sidestep has this new song out called 'Stepping to the Beat' that's just awesome," Katie suggested.

"That's a fun song," I said. I began to dance, singing Sidestep's song. "We're stepping to the beat. Yeah, yeah, we're stepping to the beat."

"It's kind of Top Forty, isn't it?" Randy said, wrinkling her nose up a little.

"That's good, though, right?" Al asked. "That means there'll be a high recognizability factor."

"What?" I asked, wondering what she was talking about.

"A lot of people will know the song," Katie explained.

"But it's also a negative, too," Randy added. "I mean, we get judged on our originality, right? How original is a song that everyone knows?"

"That's true," I agreed. "We don't want to do something that someone else might do. We have to do something totally different."

"How about 'Kick It' by the Posse," Randy suggested.

"The Posse!" I exclaimed. "That's a rap group!"

"They're not just a rap group, Sabs," Randy said. "They're the hottest rap group in history. They're also one of the few female rap groups around today."

"I don't know if I can dance like that," Katie said. I was secretly relieved. I didn't know how to dance like that either, but I didn't want to say it. Luckily, Katie said it for me.

"What about 'The Secret of Life' by Lisa Durhan?" Allison asked. "Her band sings, too, so there're enough parts for everybody."

"That's a really pretty song, but it's kind of mellow, isn't it?" I asked. This was going to be even harder than I had thought. I started getting hungry again. I had really been too excited to eat dinner.

"Maybe we should take a little break and make some popcorn," I suggested. "Food for thought and all that."

Randy groaned. "You're too much, Sabs," she said, heading into the kitchen area. There are no walls anywhere in the barn, except around the bathroom. Olivia has a Chinese screen around her bedroom, and Randy's bedroom is in the loft. I love the way they've planned the space in the barn. "Are you guys helping or what?" Randy asked.

We all got up and headed into the kitchen.

"Do you think Rick Stevens eats popcorn?" Allison asked as she melted the butter.

"Sure," Katie said. "But he probably doesn't add any butter. He looks like he only eats healthy stuff. He probably works out a lot, too. He definitely looks as if he's in shape." Katie would know about that. She's an incredible athlete. She was one of the star players on the boys' ice hockey team this past year. A lot of people were really surprised when she tried out, since she had always been a flag girl and stuff. But she's incredible on the ice and scored the second-highest number of goals for the season.

"Yeah, he probably eats salad and drinks mineral water all the time," I added. I had read that lots of actors drink mineral water at parties. I tried it once and hated it. It's got kind of a funny taste to it. Not quite like tap water. I try to drink it once in a while so that I can get used to it by the time I have to go to celebrity parties.

We bought the popcorn back into the living room and thought some more about songs. All of a sudden, I knew what we could sing — something everyone would agree on. "What about The Connection? That's the group that sings 'Bounce Right Back,'" I said.

"I like that song," Randy said. "It's got a rap piece in it."

"Yeah, it's got something for everyone," I continued. "They blend rap, pop, and rock in the same song. And the words are on the album jacket cover."

"Sounds good," Katie agreed, taking a handful of popcorn.

"What about you, Allison?" I asked, turning toward her.

Allison nodded. "I like it," she said.

"Good, we're set," I said in satisfaction. I felt as if the hardest part were over and now all we had to do was practice.

"What about our costumes?" Randy asked.

"Well, we don't have to figure that out now," Allison said. "We don't need them for the auditions."

"Yeah, but if we knew what we were wearing, it would be easier to plan our dance steps and stuff," Katie brought up.

"Really," I agreed. "Besides, it's important to get in the right mood for the song. We should definitely know what we're going to wear." I thought we should wear something glamorous. I mean, this was national television and all that. I didn't want to look too young.

"We could dress up as colored balls and bounce across the stage!" Katie suggested enthusiastically.

I must have looked pretty funny for a moment. My mouth opened and shut a few times, but no sound came out. I was kind of horrified. My big moment on television and I was going to be dressed as a big rubber ball? Then I realized that there was no way anyone else would go for that idea. I really didn't think I had anything to worry about.

"That's a great theme," Al agreed. "Sounds like fun."

Again, I just looked at everyone with my mouth opening and shutting for a few seconds. Allison liked the idea of dressing up as a giant rubber ball? Well, there was no possibility Randy was going to go for it.

"Can I be a black ball?" Randy asked. "You know, like the eight ball in pool or something."

Randy wanted to be a giant black rubber ball? I couldn't believe it!

"What's the matter, Sabs?" Allison asked, looking at me closely. "You don't look happy."

"Well. . .uh. . ." I began, wanting to tell them that there was no way I'd be a rubber ball on television. But then I saw how excited they looked. I knew that they were doing this whole thing for me and everything and they didn't have to. I sighed. If they wanted to be rubber balls, rubber balls we'd be. All actresses have to start out somewhere. I once read that Peggy Lane, who is one of the hottest TV stars today, started out as a toothbrush in a toothpaste commercial.

"All right, let's do it," I said quickly, before I could change my mind. "It will show how versatile I can be in my acting," I joked, turning my nose up in the air.

"I have The Connection's tape upstairs," Randy said. "Let's play it and see how many words we know." She ran upstairs and I heard her throwing things around before she clattered back down the stairs.

She went over to the stereo next to the television, put the tape in, and pressed "Play." None of us were really sure about the words in the verses, but we had the refrain down cold.

"We're gonna bounce, bounce right back, bounce right back to you," I sang.

"No matter where you go, no matter what you do, we're gonna bounce right back to you," Randy chimed in.

"You can't push us back, as a matter of fact," Allison added.

"So hop on board, get back on track, and we'll bounce right back to you," Katie finished.

"Hey, that was pretty good," I said. Let's listen to the verses again." Just then, the doorbell rang.

"*Uno momento*," Randy called, clicking off the stereo. She opened the door and Billy Dixon, Nick, Jason, Arizonna, and my brother Sam spilled in. It was almost as if they had been leaning against the door, and they literally fell in when Randy opened it.

"Hey," Billy said, walking over to the couch and plopping down. He grabbed some popcorn and started eating it. Allison had tutored Billy as part of our school's peer tutoring program a few months ago. He has kind of a tough reputation, but he isn't really tough. I sort of think he's a little shy. He's really good friends with Sam and those guys now, especially with Arizonna. They are kind of a weird pair, but I guess they balance each other out — like Katie and I do.

"How's practicing?" Arizonna asked, going to stand behind the video camera. "This is very!"

"Cool," Sam agreed, walking next to him.

"Well, we picked our song," I said, happy to have something to report. "It's 'Bounce Right Back' by The Connection."

"That's a good song," Nick said, throwing popcorn at Billy. "I love that rap section."

"So, Sabs, are you guys going to have to raid Mom's closet for dresses and stuff?" Sam asked. As much as he teased me, I knew he was excited for me.

"Well, actually, Katie came up with a different kind of costume idea," I said. I still wasn't sure about this whole idea, but I had agreed to it already.

"We're going to dress up as giant rubber balls," Katie revealed. "Get it — bounce right back?"

"We'll be bouncing all over the stage," Randy added, showing Arizonna how to work her camera.

"Actually, four bouncing balls sounds kind of funny," Sam said. "That just might get you on the show. It's definitely different."

"It's a hot tune, don't you think, B.D.?" Arizonna asked Billy.

"Cool," Billy said, smiling at Allison. I think he has a crush on her.

"So, what kind of dance do you think you're going to do?" Jason asked. "I mean, don't you have to, like, plan it first?"

I nodded. What were we going to do? I wondered.

We all looked at each other and shrugged. I guess no one had really thought about it.

"If you're balls, babes," Arizonna said, "you should most definitely bounce."

"Bounce?" Allison asked hesitantly.

"Bounce?" I echoed. "What do you mean?"

"Kind of like slam dancing," Arizonna replied, jumping around the room. He banged into me and then into Allison. "You know, bounce into each other."

"Well, maybe we should practice it," Katie suggested hesitantly.

I really wasn't sure about this now — slam dancing as giant rubber balls? I had pictured this very differently — a sequined gown and smooth dancing and stuff.

"Well, let's tape it and see how we look," Randy added. "That way, we can see what needs help."

"I don't know how to use this thing," I said, walking behind the camera. "Oh, wait, here's the viewer. Dance for me, Katie." I focused on Katie, and Arizonna flipped the "On" button.

Katie looked a little embarrassed for a minute — she hates to have her picture taken. But then Sam jumped in front of the camera. He's as big a ham as I am.

"Work with me, babe, work with me," Sam said to Katie, walking over to her and putting his arm around her shoulders. He turned her around so that they were both facing the camera.

"Look, it's the beautiful and talented Miss Katherine Campbell!" Sam exclaimed, mimicking the host on one of those beauty shows. "Miss Campbell's hobbies include studying, lip-synching, and bashing hockey players against the wall in championship games."

We all laughed. Sam's such a cutup.

"Do you have anything to add, Miss Campbell?" Sam asked.

"Just that I'm very happy to be here," Katie replied, getting into the swing of it. Katie's a really good sport.

"Don't forget to say how much you love your country!" Randy called out. "All those contestants always say that."

"Oh, yeah," Katie said. "And I love my country."

I giggled.

"And what about you, Allison Cloud?" Sam asked, walking over to her. He held up a hand as if he were talking into a mike. "Here's the question segment of the competition."

Allison looked up expectantly. She probably knew that she could answer any question Sam would ask. Allison knows practically everything. She reads all the time. Last summer, she actually read over one hundred books!

"What do you see as the most important problem in the world today?" Sam asked, pushing Billy over on the couch and sitting down next to Al.

"Well. . ." Allison began, but Sam cut her off.

"And what would you do to solve it?" he asked, grinning and winking at me.

"I think the biggest problem in the world today is the lack of respect for our planet," Allison replied. "We're not taking care of the environment, and if we're not careful, there may be no world for us to live in when we're older."

"Good answer, good answer!" Nick and Jason yelled, clapping and cheering.

"Don't forget to say how we can solve the problem if we all work together!" Randy called out. "They always say that."

"Ah, yes," Allison replied with a wink. "But I think we can save our planet and protect the environment if we all work together," she said.

"Great, and thank you!" Sam said in his fake beauty-pageant-host voice. "And now, Miss New York, Randy Zak!"

Randy bounced out in front of the camera, next to Sam.

"Let's see your talent!" Sam continued.

Pulling her drumsticks out of her back pocket, Randy started to do a little air drumming. But then she stopped abruptly and dropped both of them.

"Oh, I forgot who I was," she said quickly. "I probably can't drum. I should be doing something like a baton routine. But I never learned how to do that so I'll just tap-dance. They always do that."

I was so surprised, I almost stopped the camera. Tap-dance!? She must be kidding, I thought. Randy couldn't tap-dance.

But she did. She just started tapping away, right there. When she finished, she threw up her arms and gave a little bow. We all must have looked kind of shocked, because she started laughing.

"What?" she asked, plopping down on the floor. "I never told you I could tap-dance?"

"Where did you learn to do that?" I asked when I could finally speak.

"Sheck and I took tap lessons when we were in fourth grade," Randy said. "One of my neighbors, this old dude, used to be a really big tapper in the fifties. Anyway, he gave us lessons. Pretty wild, huh?"

Randy's full of surprises. I could never get bored hanging around her. She's always doing something else. Tap-dancing?

As I climbed into bed later, I realized that we hadn't even worked on our bouncing dance. I still couldn't believe that I was going to have to be dressed up as a rubber ball. But the first thing we had to do was get the song memorized, otherwise we wouldn't get past the audition. And we had to get our slam-dance bouncing down, too. I fell asleep with visions of bouncing balls in my head.

Chapter Four

I woke up the following Saturday morning with butterflies in my stomach. Or maybe they were bouncing balls. Today was the day of the audition. I got up and went to my closet to pick out what I would wear. Since we weren't wearing costumes, I wanted to have something really special — something that would get us noticed. Unfortunately, I just didn't think I had anything like that in my closet.

I couldn't decide what to wear, so I decided to take a hot bath first. I let the water run as I poured in Beauty Bubbles. Beauty Bubbles makes the ultimate bubble bath. I thought that a good soak would relax me. As I settled into the tub, I looked back on our week of practice.

We met at Randy's house every night. Learning the words was pretty easy but we had trouble getting our dance routine down. We started out okay, but as the song moved along, we bounced faster. Arizonna said that we were letting the rhythm slip by. Today was the ultimate test. We hoped we would feel the beat and slam-bounce the right way.

"Hey, Sabrina, if you stay in there much longer, you'll turn into a prune!" Sam called from outside the bathroom door.

I looked at my fingers — they were beginning to wrinkle a little bit. I got out of the tub and dried off. Now it was time to check out the clothes situation again.

Finally, after I had tried on every last thing in my closet, I was as ready as I would ever be. I was wearing my new paper bag baggy jeans, with a thick black belt and a white scooped-neck, long-sleeved T-shirt. I pulled my hair back into two black-and-white-striped combs and slipped on my black flats just as my mom called for me from downstairs. She was driving us all to the audition.

"Are you ready, Sabrina?" she asked as I climbed into the car.

"I think so," I replied nervously. "I thought I'd be super excited, but I just want to get this over with." My palms were already sweating.

"Relax, Sabrina," Mom said with a smile.

"You and your friends have been working hard all week for this. Once you get in there, you'll be raring to go."

We picked up Al, Katie, and Randy.

"Gosh, I'm nervous," Katie said. "I don't think I've been this nervous since I tried out for the hockey team."

"I'm pretty anxious myself," Allison said. "My mom tried to get me to eat breakfast, but I couldn't swallow anything."

"You all look great," my mom said as she pulled up in front of Patterson High School. "Break a leg in there. I'll be back at four o'clock to take you home."

I knew we looked good, too. Randy was wearing all black — as usual. Black's her favorite color. She had on black peg-legged jeans, her black cowboy boots, and a black cro-cheted sweater over a black tank top.

Katie was wearing a denim miniskirt with a cropped turquoise sweater that matched her turquoise socks perfectly. Katie always match-es, right down to her hair bands.

In her indigo work shirt and black leggings, Allison looked great. Her long black hair hung down her back and was held in place with a beautiful turquoise barrette.

We left the car and went into the building. We weren't sure where the auditorium was, but it didn't matter. We only had to follow the crowd and we'd find it.

"Look at this scene!" Randy exclaimed, whistling. "There have to be over two hundred people here."

She was right. Everywhere you turned, it was wall-to-wall people. And was it noisy! It must have been nervous energy or something.

"I hope they have a big auditorium," Allison said. "I wonder where the producers are going to put everybody."

"There's no way the auditions will be done by four o'clock," Katie said. "We'll be here all night!"

"Hey, do you think Rick Stevens is here?" I asked. I had forgotten about the crowd for a minute and was craning my neck to find the host.

"I doubt it," Randy said. "I don't think he would show up for the auditions. There are too many people here."

"May I have your attention, please?" A voice was blaring over a bullhorn from somewhere. "We are going to try to do this as quickly as we can. There are six tables set up at the far end of the room. An assistant at the table will give you a form to fill out. Please fill out one form per group. Give your group a name to be identified by. Then list all your names on the form, along with addresses and phone numbers. As soon as you are done, please take a seat in the auditorium. We will audition the groups in numerical order. The form that you fill out will have a number at the top. When we call your number, you're on."

Then the huge group of people began moving toward the tables. "Ohmygosh," I said. "What are we going to call ourselves? We haven't even thought about it. This is terrible! We have to have a name. How come we didn't think of this?"

"Don't worry, Sabs," Randy said. "Look at these lines. It's going to take us a half hour just to get to the table."

I looked around. Randy was right. The line was not moving that fast at all. In fact, I felt as if we were in slow motion or something. We had plenty of time.

"Do you see Stacy?" Katie asked, craning

her neck.

"No, but I'm sure she's here somewhere," I answered. "Knowing her, she's probably at the front of the line."

Suddenly, a bunch of people started screaming off to the right side. "Rick Stevens must be here!" I exclaimed, thinking that that was the only reason anybody would have for screaming.

"I don't think it's anything," Allison said. Being tall was a definite advantage for her. She could see over almost everyone's head. "I think that a bunch of girls ran into some friends of theirs. I don't see any signs of Rick."

Al must have been right, because there were no more loud screams after that. The noise just kind of leveled off.

"So, what are we going to call ourselves?" Katie asked.

"What about something like the Supremes?" I asked. "I mean, the name means the best and that's what we're going to be."

"But that name's already taken," Allison pointed out.

"I meant something like it," I replied.

"What about The Most Excellents?" Randy

asked, grinning at me. We all giggled. Arizonna would like something like that.

"Or we could be The Verys," Katie added.

We cracked up again. Unfortunately, this was getting us nowhere. We had to come up with something — soon.

"Guys," I said nervously. "We're getting closer to the front of the line. What are we going to do?"

"How about On the Edge?" Randy suggested seriously. She had been a deejay on the high school radio station a while back for a couple weeks and she had called herself the Cutting Edge. That's probably where she got the name.

"I like that!" I exclaimed. "On the Edge! We're right on the edge of . . . the edge of what?"

"Coolness," Randy replied quickly. "Well, I guess we'd have to be over the edge of coolness, otherwise we'd be not quite cool."

"Over the Edge?" Katie asked, wrinkling her nose. "I don't know if we want to call ourselves that."

"I agree," Allison said. "We want a name that's positive, right?"

We all nodded. Moving up another few

places in line, I noticed that there were only two groups in front of us now. We had better hurry or we'd be nameless. There's no way we'd get on "Hitline U.S.A." without a name.

"What about something like Pump It Up?" Allison suggested thoughtfully.

That girl is full of surprises. That was a great name! It definitely wasn't something I'd expect Allison to think of, because she doesn't listen to the radio or anything. But I thought it was perfect.

"I love it!" I exclaimed enthusiastically.

"Me too," Katie agreed, patting Al on the back. "Good idea."

"What about you, Randy?" I asked. I knew that we were almost at the front of the line and had to have a name right at that moment. But I also knew that we had to have a name that we all liked, no matter what.

"I think it's cool," Randy said, grinning at Al. "I couldn't have come up with a better name myself."

Perfect timing. We were at the head of the line. We filled out the form and headed into the auditorium. Our number was thirty-seven, so we probably hadn't been as far back in the line as I had thought at first.

"This is some scene," Randy said as we walked into the auditorium. We had entered at the back of the auditorium, where it was pretty dark. But the front of the hall was filled with bright lights.

We sat down in the middle of the auditorium. All around us, people were talking about the TV set. There was a neon sign over the stage that said "Hitline U.S.A." There were director's chairs and video cameras set up all over the front of the room.

"Those cameras are huge," Katie said. "They're taller than the guys operating them."

"They're the real thing," Randy said. "They're probably going to record us so that the producers can pick which groups they want for the show. It's got to be hard for them to remember what the first groups were like by the time they get to the last groups. I'm glad they're taping. We've got a better chance since it looks as if we're near the beginning."

"Whew! It sure is hot in here," I said. I was already starting to sweat. "It must be all of those big lights."

"It's probably much worse on stage,"

Allison said.

"All right, we are ready to begin," a man said as he walked onto the stage. "My name is Raymond Foy and I am the producer of 'Hitline U.S.A.' I want to thank all of you for coming out here this afternoon." Everyone applauded the producer — enthusiastically.

"Remember, the judging today will be based on your lip-synching ability and dance moves," Mr. Foy said, and then he called the first group on stage.

"Do you see Stacy yet?" Katie asked about half an hour later. I was wondering where The Great was, too. I had expected her to be in the first group.

"I still don't see her," I replied, turning my attention back to the stage. It was weird. Some groups were really good, and I felt as if I were sitting at home watching the show on television. Other groups weren't so good. I hoped we fell into the good category.

Things were moving pretty quickly because they weren't judging. It was strange not knowing how anyone was really doing. The groups would come up and lip-synch to their song, and that was it. The producer would thank them and send them off the stage. "I don't think we'll get any idea if they like us or not," I muttered, feeling nervous again.

"They probably aren't even concentrating," Randy said. "That's why they're recording us." We watched the groups in silence for a while.

"That last group was great," Randy said. The last group had done B. B. Browne's rap hit "Rock the Block." "They're awesome dancers."

"Number twenty-two is up," the producer said. "The Valentines. Where's number twenty-two?" Four girls strutted onto the stage.

"Hey, look, it's Stacy!" Randy exclaimed.

Sure enough, it was definitely Stacy, Eva, B.Z., and Laurel. I couldn't believe my eyes! They were all wearing these amazing red sequined dresses, looking the way I thought we'd look if we weren't wearing rubber ball costumes. They were even wearing red satin-like high heels!

"I thought we weren't supposed to wear costumes," Katie said angrily. "They definitely don't look like they're wearing their street clothes."

"I've never seen Stacy wearing that dress to school before," I agreed. "I don't think this is very fair."

"Well, they've still got to lip-synch," Allison said. "All the costumes in the world won't help if they can't dance or don't know the words."

Unfortunately, they did know the words. And could they dance! They lip-synched to the song "Just a Heartbeat Away" by Sweet Sixteen. The Valentines kind of reminded me of the Supremes or something, the way they were all in line behind Stacy and they all did the same dance steps.

"They were great!" I exclaimed when the Valentines were done.

"They weren't bad," Randy admitted. "But we're much better. I mean, we're totally original."

We watched the next few acts in silence. No one said anything else about Stacy and the Valentines, but I knew we were all thinking the same thing. Stacy was good. It would be terrible if they made it onto "Hitline U.S.A." and we didn't.

Suddenly, our number was called. Everyone looked kind of nervous as we got up to walk toward the stage. I felt this quick flash of anger. We shouldn't be nervous. We were good. We were better than Stacy and the Valentines.

"Hey, guys!" I said, stopping them. "Listen, we're good! We don't have anything to worry about. Let's just go up there and have fun!"

Randy grinned. "Sabs is right," she agreed. "Let's go kick it!"

"Pump it up!" I exclaimed.

"Let's do it!" Katie added as Allison nodded her agreement.

I felt better now. We were ready. After we got on stage, we handed our tape to the guy by the stereo. A moment later the voices of The Connection came on loud and clear through a pair of big speakers in front of the stage. We all started dancing and lip-synching to the music. "We're gonna bounce, bounce right back, bounce right back to you." It was weird to open your mouth and pretend to sing, but I started getting into it. Before I knew it, the song was over.

"We were great!" Katie exclaimed. The audience must have agreed because we heard applause throughout the auditorium.

"Thank you, girls," the producer said. "Exit through the back of the stage. I'll be in touch." That was it. We turned and walked off the stage. A woman at the door gave us each a "Hitline U.S.A." T-shirt. It was kind of cute because it had Rick Stevens's face in the corner.

"I think we have a good shot at getting on the show," I said. "I think our timing was much better than it was at our last practice."

"I think so, too," Katie said.

"I wonder if we're going to hear if we don't make it," Allison said.

"I think you only hear if you do make it," Randy replied.

"So when do you think we'll find out?" Katie asked as we walked over to my mother's car.

"I don't know," I said, shrugging my shoulders. "But we will hear from them," I said. "I know we will." At least, I hope we will, I thought to myself.

Chapter Five

"Look, girls. It's Pump It Up," Stacy said snidely as she and her friends approached my locker the following Monday right before lunch. Al, Katie, and Randy were with me. "Have you heard anything from Raymond Foy yet?"

My heart skipped a beat. Somehow I knew that she wasn't asking just to ask. She must have heard. Otherwise why would she bring it up? I didn't say anything, wishing Stacy would just go away.

"We did," Stacy continued. "Ray called my house personally. He said that the Valentines would be on next week's show. I'm sure that he's made all of his calls, so if you haven't heard by now. . ." Stacy trailed off as her friends giggled.

"How did you find out, Stacy?" Allison asked, not sounding as if she believed Stacy.

"We've been in school all morning." Allison was right. Maybe Stacy was just trying to psych us out. I wouldn't put it past her.

"Well, Ray called my house, and my mother took the message," she said, tossing her hair over her shoulder as she paused. "Then my mother called my dad. Dad had me called down to his office in the middle of my class. I actually thought that maybe I was in trouble. You know, getting called to the principal's office in the middle of class." Stacy started giggling again. I rolled my eyes. Like Stacy would get in trouble with her father, the principal of the school. Right.

"Hee, hee, hee," Randy giggled, sounding just like Stacy. Then Randy did her patented, famous "Stacy Flip" with her hair. She tossed her hair over her shoulder, just like Stacy does. Randy could imitate Stacy perfectly. Of course, Stacy's so wrapped up in herself, she didn't even notice. I grinned at Randy and gave her a thumbs-up.

"Anyway, my dad gave me the message about the show," Stacy continued as if Randy had not made a sound. "Too bad you didn't make it. I'm sure you did your best. I'll see if I can get you tickets to come see the show, if you'd like. Well, ciao for now."

Stacy flipped her hair one last time — rather strongly. The ends hit me right in the face. Then she and her friends took off toward the cafeteria, laughing.

We all stood there, a little in shock. Stacy had made it onto "Hitline U.S.A." It wasn't fair. We had worked so hard!

"Hey, Sabs," Katie said after a moment. "Let's call our houses and see if there are any messages. You never know, maybe he has called us and we just don't know it."

"You're right, Katie," I said, feeling a little better. I mean, how was he going to call us at school? "Let's go to the phones."

But there were no messages at any of our houses. We all tried to act as if it didn't matter, but I don't think it was really working. As soon as we sat down at a table with Arizonna, Nick, Jason, and Sam, they knew something was wrong.

"Babes, what's the prob?" Arizonna asked.

"It doesn't have anything to do with 'Hitline U.S.A.,' does it?" Nick asked, looking at me closely.

"No way, dude!" Arizonna exclaimed. "I heard you did some serious kicking at the audition."

"How did you hear that?" I asked curiously. For a minute, I thought he knew something that we didn't.

"Sam told me," Arizonna replied.

I spun around and stared at Sam. His face was almost as red as his hair, and he was staring very intently at his sandwich, as if it was the most interesting thing in the world. I knew that Sam stuck up for me when I wasn't around, but I didn't know it went this far. Of course, he denied it to my face. Guys. I'll never understand them.

"I didn't say you kicked," Sam protested. "I just said you said that you thought it went well."

I nodded, not believing him. Arizonna had probably quoted him exactly. It sounded like something Sam would say. I didn't really care at that moment if we never heard from Raymond Foy. I knew that our friends and family supported us, and I guess that's all that really mattered.

"The Valentines heard from 'Hitline

U.S.A.,'" Katie said. I guess she figured we might as well get it over with. The guys were going to hear about it sooner or later.

"Most excellent," Arizonna said in satisfaction. I looked at him in disbelief, feeling a little bit hurt.

"What?" I asked him when I could finally talk.

"Coolness," Arizonna replied. "It's very. They worked hard on that dance."

"How do you know?" Randy asked, her eyes narrowing a little. "Did you help them out?"

"Most definitely. They kept asking me to help and you guys were doing great already. You didn't need me." Arizonna answered her with a laugh.

"How could you?" I cried, forgetting for a moment that the guys can't see what a phony Stacy is.

"But she kept asking me," he replied simply.

"Dude, you shouldn't have done it," Billy said as he put his tray next to Allison's and sat down. "It's like you were helping the competition."

Billy is the only guy I know who sees the

true Stacy. Well, I guess Randy's friend Sheck from New York does, too. But he doesn't live here, so he doesn't really count. Anyway, Stacy can be kind of snobby toward Billy, because he's kind of tough and everything. She thinks she's better than him. What else is new?

Arizonna looked a little confused. I guess he hadn't even thought about the fact that we were competing with Stacy.

"Don't worry about it, Zone," Randy said. She had obviously had the same thought I had. "You couldn't know that we wouldn't make the show and Stacy would."

"You guys didn't make it?" Nick asked in shock. "Are you sure?"

"Well, Stacy got the call already," I pointed out. "And we didn't."

The guys looked so upset that I giggled. I mean, we were the ones who should be depressed, not them. And suddenly, I didn't feel all that bad.

"Hey, guys," Randy said. "Don't worry about it."

"Really," I agreed. "I mean, it was fun trying out and everything."

"Yeah, it's no big deal," Katie added.

"Before you know it, we'll be doing something else," I added. I decided that when I got home, I would look in the current *Young Chic* to see if there were any new contests — anything to take our minds off "Hitline U.S.A."

The guys were all right after that. I guess they just didn't want to see us upset about anything. Anyway, the day flew by after lunch. I kind of thought I'd keep obsessing about "Hitline U.S.A.," but I didn't. Not even after I saw Stacy — who I think went out of her way to see me — and she kept saying, "I'm so sorry, Sabs. Maybe next time." Like she was really sorry.

For a few minutes during band, I wondered if maybe the Valentines made it onto the show because of their costumes. I mean, they had looked so incredibly glamorous with their sequins, high heels, makeup, hair, and everything. And there we were — bouncing all over the stage. The contrast must have been startling. I knew they were looking for young acts, but maybe they wanted old young acts, like Stacy's. Then I figured there was no use talking about what-ifs. They hadn't called. We hadn't made it. That was all there was to it.

When I got home, I checked for messages again, just in case. Nothing. I wanted to call Al, Katie, and Randy to see if they had heard anything, but I figured they would have called me if they had. So I just went up to my room and started my homework. The next thing I knew, it was time for dinner.

"So, did you hear about 'Hitline U.S.A.'?" my dad asked as soon as we all sat down to dinner.

I guess my mother hadn't told him that we hadn't. "No, Dad," I replied. "Stacy and her group heard this afternoon, but we didn't. I guess we just weren't good enough."

All of a sudden, my brother Luke coughed wildly. "Oh, my gosh, Sabrina," he said when he caught his breath. "I forgot to tell you. Some guy named Goy or Hoy or Joy called for you this afternoon."

"You mean Foy!?" I practically shouted across the table at him.

"Yeah, I think that's it," he said. "I wrote his number down somewhere."

"Where!?" I asked, leaping out of my seat. Raymond Foy had called. That must mean we had made it. I hoped it wasn't too late to call him back.

"Let me think about it," Luke said slowly, scratching his head.

"Of course, you didn't use those message pads I bought, did you?" Mom asked with a sigh. She's forever telling us to write everything down, and she even leaves message pads by the phone. But it doesn't do much good.

"No-oo," Luke replied slowly. "Hmmm."

"Well, what were you doing when you answered the phone?" I asked, hoping to track the number down that way.

"I was on my way to shoot some hoops with Mark," Luke said, looking at my brother Mark.

"Oh, yeah!" Mark said, as if he suddenly remembered something. "You grabbed the pen and. . ."

"And what?" I asked, totally losing my patience. "Where did you write it?"

Luke grinned at me, but I couldn't see what was so funny.

"What?" I demanded.

"Do you want it attached to me, or would you like to be able to carry it to the phone?" he asked, still grinning.

"What are you talking about?" I asked, not having any time for games. What if Raymond Foy decided he couldn't wait for us and called another group instead?

Luke reached down under the table. A few seconds later, he held up his basketball sneaker. "I wrote it on the side of my shoe," he said. "I couldn't find any paper."

My mom rolled her eyes at me. Couldn't find any paper? Those message pads were hanging right next to the chalkboard, next to the phone.

I grabbed Luke's shoe. "Did he say how late I could call him?" I asked, heading for the phone in the kitchen.

"Something about six o'clock, L.A. time," Luke replied.

L.A. time, I thought to myself. That sounded so incredibly cool. I hoped I wasn't too late. I hoped we could still get on the show. I took a deep breath and picked up the phone.

Chapter Six

(Sabrina calls Raymond Foy.)

WOMAN: Good afternoon. Foy Productions.

SABRINA: Hi. I mean, hello. Can I . . . May I
speak to Mr. Raymond Foy,
please?

WOMAN: Who's calling?

SABRINA: This is Sabrina Wells . . . Oh! And
I'm returning his call.

WOMAN: One moment, please. Let me see if
he's in.

*(There is a pause while the woman puts Sabs on
hold.)*

RAYMOND: Hello, Sabrina. How are you?

SABRINA: Fine, thank you, Mr. Foy. I'm
sorry I missed your call. Are we
on the show?

(Raymond laughs.)

RAYMOND: Whoa! You get right to the point, don't you? I like that. Definitely, Sabrina. We really liked Pump It Up, and we'd like to invite you to be on the show. Oh, and call me Ray, okay?

SABRINA: Seriously? Really? Ohmygosh! You want us on the show? Ohmygosh! That's great, Mr. Foy! I mean, Ray.

RAYMOND: I'm glad to hear you're so enthusiastic about it. We have a feeling this is going to be a great show.

SABRINA: Ohmygosh! I've got to call my friends. Thanks a lot, Mr. Foy. I mean, Ray.

RAYMOND: Hold up, Sabrina. You are wired! I have to tell you where and when the taping is going to be held.

SABRINA: Oh, yeah. I forgot about that.

RAYMOND: We rented a studio in Minneapolis called Sound Around. Is it going to be a problem for you to get there? If it is, let me know. We can probably arrange for a car to come pick you up.

SABRINA: No problem. Great! Thanks a lot!

(Raymond laughs.)

RAYMOND: Don't you want to know what time?

SABRINA: Oh, yeah.

RAYMOND: We start taping this Saturday at one o'clock sharp. Try to get there an hour or so early so you can get into costume and do anything else you have to do.

SABRINA: Great.

RAYMOND: So, we'll be seeing you then. If you have any questions, or problems before then, you can call me back at this number between eleven and six, L.A. time.

SABRINA: Oh, wait! I have a question. Do you think you could tell me who the celebrity panelist is going to be? I mean, I'm about to die. I can't wait to find out!

RAYMOND: Well, it's supposed to be a surprise, but for you, Sabrina . . . It's Alek Carreon.

SABRINA: Alek Carreon?! No way!
Ohmygosh! He is so incredibly
gorgeous! Oh, I can't wait.

RAYMOND: I'm glad to hear that. Alek hap-
pens to be a good friend of mine.
Now remember, it's a secret.

SABRINA: Thank you very much, Ray. I definitely appreciate it.

RAYMOND: I'll see you Saturday, Sabrina.
And good luck.

SABRINA: Thank you. Thank you. Good-
bye!

(Sabrina calls Katie.)

KATIE: Campbell and Beauvais resi-
dence, Katherine speaking.

SABRINA: I bet you still can't get used to
saying that, right?

KATIE: Oh, hi, Sabs! No, it's still kind of
weird. Mom's only been married
to Jean-Paul for a little while. I'm
sure I'll get used to it soon.
What's up?

SABRINA: Katie, he called! He actually
called!

KATIE: Who called?

SABRINA: Raymond, Foy!

KATIE: Seriously? What did he say?

SABRINA: We did it! We're in. We're on the
            show. We're taping in
            Minneapolis on Saturday. We'd
            better get working on our
            costumes and everything.

KATIE: Wow! That's great! I really didn't
            think we had made it. Stacy is
            going to be pretty mad when she
            hears.

SABRINA: I hope I'm there when she finds
            out so I can see her face. Better
            yet, if Randy has her video cam-
            era, she can get her reaction on
            tape and we can watch every so
            often, just to make us feel good.

(Katie laughs.)

KATIE: Sabs, you're terrible!

SABRINA: I know. But it is funny, isn't it?
            Listen, there's more. Ray said it
            was a secret, but I can tell you
            guys. I mean, I have to tell some-
            body. I'm about to burst. I think

	Rick Stevens is cute, but this is too much. He is too incredibly beautiful. It can't be real. I'm going to die.
KATIE:	Slow down, Sabs. What's the big secret? And who is incredibly gorgeous?
SABRINA:	The celebrity guest is Alek Carreon!
KATIE:	Wow! I loved him in *Down Under*. That was a great movie and he was fantastic in it.
SABRINA:	Yeah. He won best supporting actor. I love his Australian accent. And he is sooo cute!
KATIE:	Sabs, this is going to be great! We have to get together tomorrow and work on our costumes.
SABRINA:	Definitely. Listen, I'm going to call Al and Randy. I don't want to keep them in suspense any longer.
KATIE:	Okay. I'm going to look around tonight and see if I have anything we can use for our costumes. I'll talk to you in school.

SABRINA: Okay. Wait! I almost forgot to tell
            you this, too. Ray said that if we
            couldn't get a ride to the studio,
            he would send a car to pick us
            up. Do you think he meant a
            limo? That's what they always
            call it in all those movies about
            Hollywood.

KATIE: He was going to send a limo to
            pick us up? This whole thing is
            just starting to sink in. This is *so*
            exciting!

SABRINA: Yeah! I'd better get going. Allison
            and Randy are going to be so
            psyched! Bye, Katie. Gosh, I hope
            I can sleep tonight. I'm just *so*
            excited, too!

(Katie laughs again.)

KATIE: I'm sure you'll be able to, Sabs.
            Good night.

(Sabrina calls Randy.)

RANDY: What's up? You've got me in full
            effect!

SABRINA: Randy?

RANDY: Sabs! What's going on? The producer called and we're on the show, right?

SABRINA: How did you know?

RANDY: I knew if Stacy made it, there was no way we couldn't have. I knew we were good. Plus, you sound as if you're about to burst.

SABRINA: I am. This is incredible. We're taping in Minneapolis on Saturday.

RANDY: This is great! We'd better get motoring on our costumes. We don't have much time.

SABRINA: I know, I know. Katie said she's going to look around her house for things we can use. We should meet after school tomorrow and get started.

RANDY: Good plan. We should probably meet here, in case we need any art stuff, you know?

SABRINA: Oh, yeah.

RANDY: Listen, I'd better jam. Sheck is supposed to call me later, and I don't want to tie up the phone.

It's cool that he leaves messages during the day when he's going to call. Otherwise, I'd always miss his calls. But you know how guys are.

SABRINA: That reminds me. You won't believe this, but Luke had Ray's phone number in L.A. written on his sneaker!

RANDY: His sneaker!?

SABRINA: Don't ask. It's best not to know.

RANDY: That bad, huh?

SABRINA: Worse.

RANDY: I guess sometimes I should be thankful I'm an only child.

SABRINA: Right. Say hi to Sheck from me, okay?

RANDY: Not a problem. I'll see you mañana.

SABRINA: Okay. Ohmygosh! I almost forgot. I'm not supposed to tell anyone, but I guess it's okay to tell you, Al, and Randy. The celebrity guest is going to be Alek Carreon.

RANDY: Hey! That's cool. He's a great actor. He's not hard on the eyes either.

SABRINA: You mean he's totally cute, right?

RANDY: Most definitely. Gotta jam, Sabs. Ciao.

SABRINA: Bye.

(*Sabrina calls Allison.*)

MRS. CLOUD: Hello?

SABRINA: Mrs. Cloud? This is Sabs. Is Allison there?

MRS. CLOUD: Hello, Sabrina. How are you?

SABRINA: Fine, thanks. I've got some great news for Allison.

MRS. CLOUD: Is this about "Hitline U.S.A."?

SABRINA: It sure is.

MRS. CLOUD: Did you girls get on the show?

SABRINA: Yes! I just found out!

MRS. CLOUD: Congratulations! Allison is going to be very excited. Hold on for a moment.

ALLISON: Hi, Sabs. Mom said you

had some good news?

SABRINA: I have great news.
Raymond Foy called and
we're on the show!

ALLISON: Really? Sabs, that's incredible! But wait a minute. Why
didn't we get a message
when Stacy did?

SABRINA: We did, but Luke took the message and forgot to tell me.

ALLISON: Oh.

SABRINA: Anyway, we're on the show! Ray
said that we have to go to
Minneapolis for the taping.

ALLISON: They're taping the show? I don't
know why, but I guess I thought
it was live.

SABRINA: I never thought about it. Besides,
we can get home in time to watch
ourselves on television if they
tape it.

ALLISON: That's great.

SABRINA: I'm going to make my dad tape
this. I can use it with my portfolio
when I go to Hollywood. This is
great! So, "Hitline U.S.A." rented

a studio in Minneapolis and taping starts at one. We have to be
there an hour earlier so we can
get into our costumes and everything.

ALLISON: Our costumes! We haven't even
started them yet.

SABRINA: I know. I'm panicking. We're
going to meet at Randy's tomorrow to get started. I didn't want
to say anything to Katie because it
was her idea, and Randy had to
get off the phone, but do you really think we should be rubber
balls? I mean, Stacy and the
Valentines are so glamorous-look-
ing. And this is national television, after all.

ALLISON: I think it's a unique idea.
Anybody can wear a sequined
dress and high heels.

SABRINA: I kind of want to.

ALLISON: Well, if you don't want to dress
up as rubber balls, we definitely
should talk about it tomorrow.
We don't want to start our cos-

tumes and then change our minds.

SABRINA: I don't want to cause problems.

ALLISON: But everybody should be happy.

SABRINA: I guess. Ohmygosh! I almost forgot to tell you, too!

ALLISON: Tell me what?

SABRINA: The celebrity panelist is Alek Carreon. Can you believe it?

ALLISON: Oh, that's great. I really loved him in *Down Under*. He's very talented.

SABRINA: Not to mention incredibly good-looking. Listen, I'd better get to work on my homework. I haven't even started those word problems for math yet.

ALLISON: Okay, I'll see you tomorrow.

SABRINA: Great. And don't forget, we're working on our costumes tomorrow at Randy's house.

ALLISON: All right. Good night.

SABRINA: Bye.

Chapter Seven

"All right, Pump It Up, we have a lot of work to do," I said, clapping my hands together, like I had seen dance instructors do in the movies. "We can't let the Valentines show us up!" I put the tape in Randy's stereo and turned toward my friends. We were meeting at Randy's, just like we had planned the night before.

"That's for sure," Randy agreed. "Man, did you hear how she yelled when she heard we made it on the show, too?" Stacy had heard right after homeroom. Supposedly, she had been pretty mad — and loud. She loves to be the center of attention and she definitely wasn't anymore.

"Arizonna told me," I replied, giggling. "It must have been great. I'm sorry I missed it."

"Me too," Randy agreed.

"Maybe we should get to work on our costumes first and practice dancing later," Allison suggested. "After all, we were good enough to get on the show but we have no costumes."

"That's true," I replied. "But we can't let ourselves get lazy. All the other groups have had a whole extra day to practice. They knew they were on the show yesterday."

"So, what about the costumes?" Katie asked. "I talked to my mom about them, and when I got home from school, she had left this bag on my bed for us." She dumped the contents of a large shopping bag out onto the floor. Suddenly, there were pink rubber balls bouncing around all over the place. "They're perfect," Katie told us enthusiastically. "Mom said we could cut them in half and sew them on our costumes. They're hollow, like tennis balls, so it won't be hard at all."

It suddenly looked as if it was too late to talk about changing the costumes. I mean, if Mrs. Campbell — oops, I meant Mrs. Beauvais — had gone to all this trouble and actually bought stuff, it looked as if I had no choice but to be a rubber ball. I tried not to let my disappointment show. Everyone else was so excited about the whole thing.

"Check this out!" Randy exclaimed, walking over to her mother's studio in the back of the barn. "I was talking to M about our costumes last night, and she started talking about living sculpture and all this other stuff."

"Living sculpture?" I asked, feeling nervous. I had seen some of Olivia's sculptures. They're really cool and definitely wild, but they're kind of big. I didn't think I could wear one. And if we weren't going to wear them, how would they be living? I had a feeling I didn't want to know the answer. It definitely didn't sound like glamorous sequins or anything.

"Right," Randy replied. "And then she went and made these. You know, I totally forgot that she knows how to sew."

"Your mom knows how to sew?" Katie asked in a kind of shock. Olivia doesn't usually go in for domestic-type things. I don't think she knows how to cook at all. Randy does most of the cooking and a lot of the grocery shopping, too. Olivia gets pretty wrapped up when she's doing art stuff and totally forgets about eating. Luckily, Randy's really into cooking, and she even says she likes to shop. That way, she can buy the food she likes to eat instead of eating the food that Olivia buys. I guess things are really different in New York City. Randy says that before her parents got divorced they used to have a cleaning woman in their apartment who would cook occasionally. They practically lived on take-out food after the divorce. Acorn Falls isn't big on take-out. We have a Chinese place and a pizza place. But that's about it. I think that was a big adjustment for Randy when she moved here.

"Yeah," Randy answered. "She had to learn when she was taking all these fashion designing courses before I was born. I guess they had to make all their own designs. She even has a sewing machine."

"Fashion design?" I asked, suddenly sidetracked. "That sounds like fun." Designing clothes sounded really cool. I hate it when I go to try on clothes and nothing fits right, or the colors aren't what I want or they're just too expensive. If I could design my own clothes, I would always love them. Maybe I should think about doing something like that as a side career — when I have downtime as an actress.

"I think it was a lot of work," Randy replied

replied matter-of-factly. "She thought they were some of the hardest courses she ever took. Anyway, this is what she made."

Randy handed each of us this large piece of fabric that looked kind of like a sheet. Hers was black, mine was red, Al's was blue, and Katie's was yellow.

"We're wearing sheets?" I asked, feeling confused. That would make us look more like colored ghosts instead of bouncing balls.

"Well, M dyed all the fabric, so the color is brighter," Randy pointed out. "And if you'll notice there's elastic on the top and the bottom, and armholes near the top. M worked all day on these." She stepped into hers and popped her arms out. The top elastic band went around her neck and the bottom was just above her knees. The whole middle part was really loose. There was a lot of fabric there.

"You don't quite look like a ball," Katie said, obviously trying to be diplomatic.

"Well, maybe a deflated ball," I added, hoping Randy's feelings wouldn't be hurt.

"Oh, that's the beauty of these things," Randy said, picking up a few pillows. She tugged open the bottom band and stuffed the pillows into the sheet. The costume started to look a little puffy. "They can be stuffed, so we look round."

"Great!" Katie exclaimed enthusiastically. "These are really great. We can use anything to stuff them, right?"

"Your mother is so talented," Allison added. She got up to try on her sheet.

"Most definitely," Randy agreed. "You can stuff them with pillows, paper, dirty laundry."

"Yuck!" Al, Katie, and I said together.

"Just kidding," Randy replied. "Anyway, we'll definitely look like bouncing balls, and our costumes are even kind of comfortable. Aren't you going to try yours on, Sabs?"

With a sigh, I stood up, too. "I feel like a fitted sheet," I said after I had it on. "Or a mattress pad."

"I think you look cute," Katie said.

"I don't want to look cute," I complained. "I want to be glamorous." I couldn't help it. They were all so excited. But I wasn't. I really didn't want to be a bouncing ball.

"You think we should change our costumes?" Katie asked. "I thought you liked my idea."

"Well. . ." I began, not wanting to hurt her feelings.

"I think Sabs just pictured us wearing something different, that's all," Allison cut in.

"Yeah, something with sequins or fringe or something," I said enthusiastically. "You know how The Connection dresses? Something like that."

"But that's so ordinary," Randy replied. "I thought the whole point was to be different. This is definitely different."

"It sure is," I agreed.

"Well, what do you guys think?" Katie asked softly. "Everyone has to like our costumes. Does anyone have any other ideas?"

"But you guys already went to all this trouble and everything," I protested. I was kind of sorry I had brought up the whole thing, now. "And Randy's mom sewed these sheets and Katie's mom bought all of those pink rubber balls."

No one said anything for a moment. I sighed because I knew I had no choice. These were my best friends, and they liked the idea of dressing up like bouncing balls. Besides, I had talked them into the whole audition. It was only fair that we wore the costumes they liked.

"Don't worry about it, guys," I said. "I'm sure I'll get used to these costumes. Besides, it is different. And we don't want to look just like the Valentines."

"That's right," Randy agreed. "We're going to score off the charts on originality."

"We sure are!" Katie replied. "This is going to be great!"

I was glad they were so enthusiastic, but I still couldn't help thinking it would be better if we were wearing sequins. It was getting pretty close to dinnertime, so we decided to meet at my house the next day after school. I walked home, carrying the costumes and a shopping bag full of rubber balls and trying to forget how glamorous the Valentines had looked.

"If it isn't a bouncing ball," a snide voice said behind me as I opened my locker the next morning. "Isn't that just the cutest thing."

"What are you talking about?" I whirled around to face Stacy. She was standing there in a lime green minidress and lime green heels. I think she's got heels in every single color. It's unbelievable. Mom says I can't get heels until I'm sixteen. She says that they aren't good for growing legs and backs. I don't really know what she's talking about.

"Oh, in the television business, nothing is private," Stacy said with a flip of her hair. "Your costumes are not exactly a big-time secret, you know. But maybe you should have kept them secret."

Eva and Laurel cracked up.

"It takes more than fancy clothes to win on 'Hitline U.S.A.,'" I said angrily. "We're going to dance you right off the stage."

"Bounce us off, you mean?" Stacy retorted, laughing. "Please. We're talking glamour here. I'm afraid to say, Sabs, that you just don't have any."

"Please," I shot back. "And you do? That's the biggest laugh I've had in a long time."

"When we win," Stacy continued as if I hadn't even spoken, "I'll be sure to invite you to the big party that we throw. That way you can say that you hung out with a celebrity."

"What will you do, pay a real celebrity to be there?" I asked, getting into it now. I never let Stacy push me around.

"Sabrina," Stacy replied slowly, "I can see you're still too immature to deal with this. I guess I should have known by your choice of costume."

She turned and walked off down the hall with her friends trailing after her. There was no way I was going to let her have the last word, though.

"Well, I'd rather be a young, but real, bouncing ball, than an old, fake, sequin queen like you!" I yelled after her.

Turning back to my locker, I was surprised to see Allison standing there.

"Al," I said in surprise. "How long have you been there?"

"Long enough," she replied with a smile. "So, you don't want to be a sequin queen anymore?"

"Definitely not!" I said firmly. "Stacy can keep her sequins. I'm all for the bouncing balls now."

After school, I practically ran all the way home. I couldn't wait to get started on our costumes. Katie's mom had bought a bunch of pink rubber balls to go on the outfits Randy's mom had sewn — we were going to look awesome!

"Hi, Mom. I'm home!" I called as I opened the back door. I left my knapsack in the kitchen and headed for the living room, where I had left the bag of rubber balls. But when I looked in the corner, the bag wasn't there. I almost started to panic, but then I figured that Mom had moved it when she was vacuuming or something. When I turned around to look for the bag, I saw Cinnamon lying on the rug, chewing on a pink rubber ball. There was another ball on the rug beside him, and another one halfway under the couch. In fact, the whole bag of rubber balls was spread out all over the living room floor.

"Oh, no!" I gasped. I got down on my hands and knees and started gathering up the rubber balls. The more balls I found, the more worried I got. Cinnamon had chewed on every single one of them! The costumes Randy's mom had sewn were ripped — they were ruined! "Cinnamon, how could you!" I groaned, glaring at the dog.

"What did Cinnamon do this time?" Sam asked just then, coming into the living room.

When he saw me sitting in the middle of the floor, surrounded by chewed-up rubber balls, he let out a long, low whistle. "Oh, man, I guess Cinnamon decided to play fetch all by himself."

"These were the only costumes we had and now they're ruined," I moaned. "What are we going to do? Tomorrow's the contest!"

Chapter Eight

Saturday morning came a little too quickly for me. I mean, I was really looking forward to taping the show, but I really didn't think we had a chance of winning without our costumes. And it was all my fault for leaving the bag of rubber balls where Cinnamon could get at them.

I looked over at my closet, where my new costume was hanging in a clear plastic dress bag. All the moms had gotten together and sewn four minidresses for us. The only problem was that now we looked just like the Valentines—minus all of those shimmering sequins. There was no way we were going to get any points for originality. Still, we had been practicing our dancing and lip-synching every single night. We knew all the words by heart and our dancing was perfect. Allison had even come up with the perfect way to end the dance, right on the last beat. That would have to count for something.

I pulled on the silky stockings I had bought to go with my dress and put my jeans on over them. Now I wouldn't have to worry about that later. I could just see myself getting all nervous and anxious and putting a rip in my stockings as I tried to put them on. Then I'd be on national television with a run in my stockings that everyone could see! Luckily, I was planning ahead.

I picked up my dress and the bag with my shoes in it. We had all run out and bought matching shoes and stockings. The moms let us splurge a bit because they felt so badly about what had happened—and, believe it or not, they even let us get shoes with small heels. My mom also said that having everything matching would help our look. Even though my mom had said that she wouldn't let me wear heels until I'm at least sixteen, she made an exception in this case. My mom's *so* cool sometimes!

I took one last look in the mirror, holding the dress up in front of me. It was really pretty, but somehow I still wished it was covered with pink rubber balls. Once I got used to the idea, I realized it would get our act a lot of attention.

"Are you ready to go?" Dad asked me as I walked down the stairs. "We'd better leave now if we're going to get there in time."

"I'm good to go," I said.

"So, Sis, this is the big day," Sam said. "Is it the day you're going to be discovered and start on the journey to fame and fortune?" I was about to throw my new dress at him when he continued. "Hey, good luck, Sabs. You don't need a bouncing ball costume to win that contest. You'll knock 'em dead!"

"Thanks, Sam," I said with a smile growing on my face. It's eerie how my brother sometimes knows exactly what I'm thinking. I had a feeling this was going to be a good day after all. We piled into the car and headed to Sound Around in Minneapolis. I was getting so excited I could barely sit still. I hoped we didn't get stuck in any traffic because then I would have to get out of the car and run around or something. I had lots of nervous energy.

I was especially nervous about meeting Rick Stevens and Alek Carreon. I was going to be in the same room with them. What would I say?

What if they said something to me? Maybe I should have worn my good jeans. Maybe I should have spent more time on my makeup. This could be my big break. Who knows?

Before I knew it, my dad was dropping us all off at the studio. My whole family had come to watch the taping, except for Matthew, my oldest brother, who is away at college. He had called last night, though, to wish me luck. And he told me he'd definitely be watching the show on television. In fact, he said he'd get his whole dorm to watch. I kind of hoped he did, and I kind of hoped he didn't. I was supposed to go visit him sometime soon. If we did well on the show, everyone would remember me. If we didn't, they'd still remember me, but not the way I wanted them to.

I didn't see my friends but there was a sign in the lobby directing all acts to Studio One. Studio One. I felt very professional. I wondered if my friends were already there.

"Well, I'd better go," I told my family. "I'm wanted on the set." I giggled. I liked the sound of that. It was something I could get used to. I gave them my movie star wave, where I don't really move my hand that much. It's kind of the same way the queen waves.

"Go get 'em!" my brothers yelled as I walked away.

I headed for the studio. The halls were really quiet and I was surprised. I would have thought that all those people in Studio One would be making a lot of noise. When I walked in, I discovered that they *were* making a lot of noise. I realized that the studio must be soundproof. The studio was packed with the other acts and TV crew members. The stage was being swept and the seats in the audience were still empty. I spotted Katie, Randy, and Allison sitting on some couches in one of the corners offstage.

"Hi, guys. I made it!" I called out with a wave. I was glad they were already there. It would be much easier to talk to Rick Stevens or Alek Carreon if my friends were with me. "Has anything happened yet? Have I missed anything?"

"Nope, we've just been looking around," Randy said. "We saw Stacy and her friends, but they just looked down their noses at us — as usual."

"Actually, I think they looked a little nervous," Allison said.

"Really?" I asked, surprised. I didn't think Stacy got nervous about anything.

"Do you think we should get changed now?" Katie asked a moment later. "There's a dressing room right over there." She pointed to a door in the wall on our right.

"Yeah, let's go," Randy agreed. We picked up our stuff and went into the dressing room to change. When we walked in, I kind of expected to see vanity tables and big lighted mirrors, like you always see in dressing rooms in the movies. But the only pieces of furniture in this room were four folding chairs. There was also a huge closet with a full-length mirror on the door. Each of us picked a chair to put our stuff on and started to put on our dresses. Nobody said anything for a while. I think we were all pretty nervous.

When everyone was ready, I took a deep breath and stood up. "Well, here we go!" I exclaimed, taking a step toward the door.

"Just a second, Sabs," Randy said from behind me. I turned around to look at her. She was standing between Allison and Katie, her hands behind her back.

"Katie, Al, and I know how bad you've been feeling about Cinnamon ruining our rubber ball costumes," Randy began in a serious tone of voice.

"And we just wanted you to know that it doesn't matter to us," Katie chimed in.

Allison nodded. "It doesn't really matter if we win or lose. We're already going to be on television."

"And we wouldn't even be doing that if you hadn't gotten us started. So that's why we got you this," Randy finished, pulling something out from behind her back and holding it out to me.

"Wow!" I gasped. Randy was holding out an incredibly gorgeous gold jacket. "Where did you get this?"

"I found it at a thrift shop," Randy told me with a grin. "It's for luck, so hurry up and put it on.

Moving quickly, I put the jacket on over my dress and walked over to look at myself in the mirror. "Perfect," I breathed, admiring the way the gold jacket sparkled. I turned around again and looked at my best friends. "You guys are the greatest friends in the whole world!"

"If we don't get out there, we'll also be the latest friends in the world," Katie said, laughing.

The four of us walked out of the dressing room just in time to hear a loud whistle coming from the center of the room. It was Raymond Foy, the producer we had met at the audition.

"Quiet on the set!" he called out. "All right, we have five groups for this episode. This is the order. First up are the Valentines. Number two is Jimmy Z. Third up is Pump It Up. Number four is After Six. And last is Jack and Jill. Everyone got that?"

There was a chorus of "Yes" from the room. I couldn't believe that Stacy's group was going first. They got to get it over with and relax for the rest of the show. The judges would be fresh and wouldn't have anything to compare them to, so they might do really well. Then again, it might be better to go last, because everyone else will have gone already. I guess we didn't have to worry about that. We were right in the middle. We could see the first two groups and get a sense of how the judges score and stuff. And then the two groups behind us might not score so well because the judges would be tired.

"All right," Ray Foy continued. "There will be two sets of commercials. One after number two's act, and one after number four's act. Since the show is being taped, there won't be actual commercials. But that's where we'll take a quick break and freshen up the host and the panelists. We'll announce the winner and runner-up right after the last act, and the show will end. Any questions?"

"Where will we be when we're not doing our act?" a girl in a white overcoat asked. I was pretty sure she was with Jack and Jill, because the guy she was with was wearing a black overcoat. They were the only boy-girl group in the room.

"You will all stay back here," the producer said, pointing to the area where we were sitting, right off the stage. "We have a TV hooked up here so you can watch the other acts." He pointed to a TV set in the corner of the room.

"Wow," Randy whispered. "We'll be watching a TV show that's being taped right next to us. That's pretty wild."

"Okay, here's the moment you've been waiting for," Ray said. "Let me introduce the two big stars of the show. First, the celebrity panelist, Alek Carreon!" The room erupted in cheers.

"He's even more gorgeous in person!" I exclaimed. Alek was dressed in black baggy pants, a white shirt buttoned all the way up to the collar, and this wild fuchsia, orange, and yellow vest. He looked fantastic — of course.

"Thank you very much," Alek said in a quiet voice, laced with an Australian accent. "Mr. Foy has made a bit of a mistake, I'm afraid." We all hushed. I turned to my friends. We all looked at each other and shrugged. We wondered what he meant. I hoped that he didn't mean that Ray had made a mistake about him being on the show.

"You see, Mr. Foy said that he wanted to introduce the two big stars of the show," he went on. I was falling in love with the sound of his voice. I could barely move when he was talking. "I think that you are the big stars of the show. I wish you all the best of luck. Cheerio."

We all clapped as he left. "Boy, he was great!" I exclaimed as I clapped. Now I knew I was in love.

"He sure was," Katie said. "His voice sent

shivers down my spine." Katie jumped as if another shiver had gone down her spine. "And now the host of the show," Ray said, "Mr. Rick Stevens."

We cheered again as Rick Stevens walked out onto the center of the stage. He was wearing black pants with white pinstripes, a black T-shirt, and a gray blazer. He looked fantastic. I noticed that he had two women next to him. One was holding hair spray and a powder brush and the other was holding a mirror.

"Thanks, kids," he said slowly in kind of a lazy way. "Remember, this is the big time. Make sure that you're quiet on the set and follow my cues. I still don't know about having all these kids on the show, Ray. Let's hope you're right. I just don't think so, though."

"Boy, he doesn't seem very nice at all," Allison whispered to me. I nodded my head in agreement.

"I knew that you kids would all be wanting my autograph after the show," Rick continued. "And I just don't have the time. But when you leave, there will be a pile of photographs on the table. I signed them all before I got here." He walked away with his makeup women following him.

"What a loser!" Randy exclaimed. "He seems completely impressed with himself."

"Yeah, he sure does," Katie said. "I don't want a picture of him."

"Really," I agreed. "His ego is so inflated, it's a wonder his head fits in the frame."

"Do you think he goes anywhere without the makeup women?" I wondered out loud.

"Probably not," Randy replied. "They're probably waiting for him as soon as he steps out of the shower in the morning."

"I don't think so," I said with a grin. "I don't think he could take a shower without makeup. The great Rick Stevens? No way."

We all giggled.

"I can just see them following Rick down the street in a rainstorm in case his makeup runs," Randy continued.

"Or brushing his hair right after a breeze so it's never out of place," I added.

Now, I doubly hoped that we might be able to talk with Alek Carreon. At least he sounded like a genuinely nice guy.

"So, Pump It Up actually showed up," Stacy said, suddenly walking up to us. She held her shoes in her hand. I guessed even a practiced high-heel wearer like herself would have problems with those heels. They were pretty high. "It was kind of a waste of time, you know. Once the judges see our act, they'll stop the show and declare the winner."

"Good luck to you, too," Randy said as Stacy walked back to her friends. I wondered why she had even walked over to talk to us in the first place. Then I remembered what Allison had said earlier about Stacy and her friends being nervous. Maybe it was true — and maybe that's why Stacy was being so impossible.

"Good luck, Stacy," I called after her. I meant it, too. After all, we were all going to be on national television. And I suddenly realized that Stacy was probably nervous.

"Okay, ladies and gentlemen. It's showtime!" Ray exclaimed. "The Valentines and Jimmy Z. — report to the side of the stage and be ready to go. Good luck, all." He turned and hurried off toward the stage.

My friends and I turned our chairs toward the television. I was really curious to see how Stacy was going to do. I hoped she didn't trip.

Well, maybe a part of me did — but it was a small, tiny little part.

The theme music for "Hitline U.S.A." came on. And then we heard the voice of Raymond Foy. "Welcome to 'Hitline U.S.A.' For the next few weeks we will be showcasing the star quality of the young people in our country. Who knows? Maybe you'll see a young star-in-the-making!"

I sat up a little straighter in my chair. He could have been talking about me!

"But before we start," Ray continued. "Here's your host, Riiiick Stevens!"

We heard the audience applaud. My heart skipped a beat. My palms were all sweaty, and I could feel my stomach in my throat. I guessed I was getting a little nervous now. I mean, it was understandable. I had never been on television before. I felt Katie grab my hand.

"This is the big time," she said, repeating the words that Rick Stevens had used earlier. I squeezed her right back.

"It sure is, Katie," I said, feeling a little out of breath for some strange reason. "It sure is."

Chapter Nine

"There they are," Allison said, pointing to the TV screen. Stacy, Eva, Laurel, and B.Z. walked onto the stage. Their dresses looked really good under the bright lights. The sequins sparkled every time they moved. Stacy and her friends had added red elbow-length gloves and red hats to their outfit since the audition.

"Boy, they do look kind of glamorous, don't they?" Katie asked no one in particular.

"Yes, but let's see their act," I said. "You never know what can happen."

"Especially the way Eva's teetering on those heels," Randy pointed out. "I predict she's going down."

We all giggled.

"Our first group will be lip-synching to Sweet Sixteen's smash hit 'Just a Heartbeat Away,'" Rick Stevens said. "Please welcome the Valentines!"

Then the music started to play and the girls began their act. From the beginning I could see that Stacy and her friends were in trouble. In their first dance move, Stacy's ankle buckled and she stumbled into Eva. It wasn't a bad slip, but it was enough to make Stacy skip her lines. Maybe the Valentines should have worn their shoes while they were waiting to go on stage, instead of carrying them. It might have helped them to get used to them.

"She's already blown the lines," Randy said. The girls put their arms around each other and began swinging their hips. This time, Laurel forgot the words to the song. When it was her turn for her solo lip-synch, the music played but her lips didn't move. Stacy jumped in front of her and began lip-synching. It looked like that screwed up the order of their routine because B.Z. and Eva both came up to the center of the stage and bumped into each other. The song was a pretty slow love song, but they seemed to be moving way too fast out there. Then B.Z. and Eva both lip-synched to the next part of the song. The problem was that none of them were following the music — or each other.

"I can't believe how messed up they are," I said after they were finished. "They were so much better at the auditions. There's no way they will win." I felt kind of bad for Stacy. I'm sure she and her friends were looking forward to this as much as we were. They finally finished their act and Rick Stevens came to shake their hands.

"Okay, nice job, girls," Rick said in his game-show voice. All of a sudden, his smile that I had loved looked really fake. "Let's see how nice the judges were to you." The scores flashed across the screen. "For originality, a five. For presentation, a five. And for lip-synching, a four. All right, that gives you a total of fourteen. Nice job. The Valentines, ladies and gentlemen!" The audience cheered as Rick escorted them off the stage.

"I hope the next group is better!" I heard Rick hiss to Ray on the side. "I cannot work with these amateurs."

"I can't believe how hot it was out there!" B.Z. exclaimed as the Valentines walked past us. Stacy did not look happy.

"And those lights were so bright," Laurel added.

"Really," Eva agreed. "You can't even see three feet in front of you."

"Is that why you kept bumping into me the whole time?" Stacy asked her. The two of them glared at each other. I thought they were going to fight right there in front of us. But instead, Stacy spun around and stalked to the back of the room to sit down. Her friends trailed after her.

"Ohh!" Randy said after they were gone. "That was ugly."

"Seriously," I agreed.

"I hope we don't screw up," Katie said. "I'm starting to feel really nervous."

"We won't," I said confidently. "We're good and we know it."

We all giggled. That had sounded like something Rick Stevens would say. The next group came on to do their act. There was a guy dressed in a white suit with a white tie dancing on the stage. He was lip-synching to the song "The Girls Are Everywhere" by Ted McGwyn. It was an old rock and roll song, and I didn't really like it, but this guy was pretty good. He had four girls in white dresses dancing behind him.

"This guy is good," I said. "Maybe he'll get a perfect score.

"He's pretty cool," Randy said, "but it's hard to get a perfect score." When the group was finished, Rick came out to greet them while the audience applauded in the background. I even heard a few people scream. The camera focused on Alek Carreon, and he was clapping and smiling. I thought he was just too beautiful for words.

"This is Jimmy Z., ladies and gentlemen," Rick said. "Great job, Jimmy. Let's see what the judges thought." The scores flashed across the screen. I heaved a sigh of relief. At least it wasn't a perfect score. We'd have no chance of winning then. "For originality, a seven. For presentation, a seven. And for lip-synching, a ten. That gives you a twenty-four. Great job. We'll be back right after these messages."

My friends and I looked at each other. We were up next! The producer came into the room. "Okay, Pump It Up and After Six, get ready," Ray Foy said. We got up and went back to the dressing room to check our hair and freshen up the makeup we were wearing. Television really bleaches you out, so you have to wear a lot of heavy makeup. I had so much stuff on my face I felt as if I was wearing a mask!

"Wow!" Katie exclaimed. "We really do look great."

"All right, girls, you're on," the producer said after we had trooped back to the offstage studio. We huddled for one last time by the side of the stage.

"This is it," I said, trying to get everyone psyched. "Let's go bounce our hearts out!"

"Well, not quite that much," Randy added. "But let's go kick it!"

We walked out onto the stage. I couldn't believe how hot it was. Eva was right. The spotlights were blinding. Rick Stevens looked bleached. We weren't taping yet and a woman was powdering his face while he was yelling about his hair or something. We looked at each other. Rick Stevens was not a nice guy at all. I looked around at the stage. There were neon lights everywhere. The "Hitline U.S.A." sign was lit up again. On the side of the stage was the panelist table. I saw Alek Carreon talking to one of the other panelists. He caught me looking at him, and he smiled.

"Ohmygosh!" I exclaimed. "Alek Carreon smiled at me!"

"Well, that's because you've been staring at him forever," Katie said. "You're probably making him nervous!" I decided not to look at him anymore. It sure seemed as if we had been waiting to come on for a long time.

The audience seats were totally filled up. There were even spotlights on them. But I couldn't see my family or my friends anywhere. Suddenly a crew member held up an applause sign to the audience, and the audience began clapping.

"Boy, that's weird," I said. "I didn't know that the audience has to be told to clap." Television was much more complicated than I thought.

Rick Stevens walked onto the stage. "Okay, we are ready for our next act," Rick said. "This group has put a new spin on The Connection's popular song 'Bounce Right Back.' Please welcome Pump It Up!"

We walked out to the center of the stage as the audience applauded. I heard a few screams and thought they sounded a lot like my brothers.

Then the song started. As soon as I heard the music, I started to lose myself in it. I forgot where I was and that we were being taped for television and that millions of television viewers all over the country were going to be watching us. I just got into the song and the whole thing just flew right by.

"We're gonna bounce, bounce right back, bounce right back to you," I synched.

Randy joined in at the right time. "No matter where you go, no matter where you are, we're gonna bounce right back to you."

Allison bounced between Katie and Randy. I thought she was going to bounce right out of her costume. "You can't push us back, as a matter of fact," she synched.

Katie followed Allison perfectly. "So hop on board, get back on track, and we'll bounce right back to you." Then we bounced each other around to the music.

On the last beat Katie, Al, and Randy swung their arms up in the air in perfect time. The next thing I knew, we were finished. I heard lots of cheering and applause coming from the audience. I looked at my friends. They were all smiling. Rick Stevens came out to us. "Let's hear it for Pump It Up!" he exclaimed. The audience cheered louder. "Let's see what the judges have to say."

We turned to face the panel. Because the lights were so bright, I couldn't see the score. I listened to Rick read them instead. "For originality, a ten. For presentation, a seven. And for lip synching, a ten! That gives you a total of twenty-seven! Congratulations, girls. That puts you in the lead." He then herded us off the stage.

We went into the back room to watch the other acts. I let out a whoop as soon as we were back off the stage.

"That was great!" Katie screamed.

"Most excellent!" Randy yelled, giving me a high-five.

I started jumping all over the place. Now, I was really pumped, and I couldn't sit still. I wanted to go back out on stage and do it again. I was made for this!

"Did you hear that crowd cheering?" Allison asked as soon as we settled down a little.

"They went absolutely wild!" Randy exclaimed.

"Even Alek was cheering," Katie said.

"He was?" I asked in surprise. "I didn't even notice." And I hadn't, surprisingly. I was so into the whole thing that I forgot he was even there.

"I think he even clapped louder than everyone else," Katie said. We sat down to watch the next act.

"Oh, no, it's that group we loved at the audition," I said. Rick Stevens was pointing to four boys dressed in baggy purple-and-gold rayon pants and loose black shirts buttoned all the way up to the collars. The leader was wearing sunglasses.

"Here, with a tough act to follow, is After Six," Rick said. "They are performing the funk of B. B. Browne and his song 'Rock the Block.'" The guys began doing splits and flips in the air to the popular rap song. Pretty soon, the whole audience was clapping to the music.

"These guys are definitely on the cutting edge," Randy said, rocking to the music.

"How can they dance like that and still lip-synch?" Allison asked. It was true. With all the body movement they had, it was amazing that they could still lip-synch. But they did, and they looked perfect.

"I think we're in trouble, guys," Randy said. When they finished, we could hear the applause from where we were sitting.

"What a performance!" Rick exclaimed. "Let's see what our panel has to say. For originality, a nine. For presentation, a ten." We held our breath. The next score would tell us if we won, lost, or tied. "And for lip-synching, a ten. That gives you a final score of twenty-nine! You're in the lead. Nice job."

I leaned back in my chair. We had lost. After Six had beaten us by one point. There was still one more act to go, but it didn't matter now. "Cheer up, Sabrina," Allison said. "We still did really well."

"Yeah, Sabs, they loved us," Randy added. Just then After Six came into the room. The leader came up to us.

"Hi, I'm Tyler," he said. "I just wanted to let you know that you guys were wild." He smiled and gave us a thumbs-up.

"You were great," I said. It was nice of him to come up and compliment us.

"Well, we may have beaten you, but I think we've got the two best groups," Tyler said.

"Well, take it easy," he added as he walked away.

"Bye," I called after him. All of a sudden I felt better. We hadn't won, but we had done our best, and everyone knew it. Even After Six. We sat and watched the last act, Jack and Jill, the boy and girl in the overcoats. They did a song called "Enough Said" by The Mix. Their whole routine seemed really boring compared to After Six's. I began to think that we might get runner-up.

"Another good performance," Rick said when they were finished. "What do you say, judges?" Alek Carreon held up the score for the last time. "For originality, a six." Al, Randy, Katie, and I hugged each other. We had won runner-up. Even if Jack and Jill got two tens, they would still be behind us. "For presentation, a seven. And for lip-synching, a ten. That makes a total of twenty-three. Nice job. And now let's bring out the winners."

He meant us! We were the runner-up! We danced around in the back, hugging each other. The producer came running into the back. "Come on, Pump It Up, you're wanted on-stage." He turned and was gone. We hurried to the side of the stage.

"First, our runner-up," Rick said. "For a very sophisticated and original act, with a score of twenty-seven, here's Pump It Up!" We came out on stage. We could hear our families cheering from somewhere in the audience. "These girls were fantastic — Sabrina Wells, Randy Zak, Katie Campbell, and Allison Cloud — Pump It Up. Give them another hand." The audience applauded again. "As runner-up, you each get a 'Hitline U.S.A.' tote bag, a free makeover at your local mall, and a fifty-dollar gift certificate to your favorite record store. Congratulations."

We walked offstage so that Rick could introduce the winners. "Here they are, the winners, with a score of twenty-nine, for an action-filled routine, After Six!" Rick called out. The noise from the audience was deafening. After Six had definitely deserved to win. We watched as they were introduced and given a check for $5,000.

We were about to go backstage when Alek Carreon came up to us. "Hi, girls," he said with a warm smile. I thought I was going to faint. "I just wanted to let you know that your act was very professional. You definitely have a future in show business."

I wanted to say something, but I was tongue-tied. Finally Allison spoke up. "Thank you, Mr. Carreon. We had a lot of fun. Oh, we loved your movie, by the way."

"Well, thank you," he replied. "Well, I'd better go. I've got to talk to Mr. Foy. I don't want him mad at me." He let out a deep laugh. It was contagious and we all giggled. "Good luck to all of you. Good-bye." He turned and went back onstage.

"I don't believe it!" I exclaimed. "Alek Carreon singled us out. He loved our act. We're ready for show business."

"Most excellent, wouldn't you say, Sabs?" Randy asked me. "Let's just celebrate one success at a time."

I laughed. Randy was right. But I was definitely on my way to stardom. I just knew it. I could feel it.

"I wish we had won," Katie said as we packed our stuff. "The runner-up prize is never really good."

"Well, the tote bag is kind of lame," Randy said. "But we can all get a couple of free CDs — maybe four if there's a sale."

"I think the makeover will be fun," I added.

"I definitely had a *ball*," Allison said, giggling, after we got our stuff and headed into the parking lot.

"I know what you mean," I replied. "My heart was *bouncing* all over the place."

Randy groaned. "You guys are terrible."

"Let's do it one more time for the road," I said as I grabbed Al and Katie's arms and hooked my arm through theirs. Randy hooked onto Al. We all began singing, "We're gonna bounce, bounce right back, bounce right back to you."

LOOK FOR THE AWESOME GIRL TALK BOOKS IN A STORE NEAR YOU!

TALK BACK!

TELL US WHAT YOU THINK ABOUT GIRL TALK

Name _____

Address _____

City _____ State _____ Zip _____

Birthday Day _____ Mo. _____ Year _____

Telephone Number (____) _____

1) On a scale of 1 (The Pits) to 5 (The Max),
how would you rate Girl Talk?   Circle One:

        1   2   3   4   5

2) What do you like most about Girl Talk?

___Characters___Situations___Telephone Talk

Other _____

3) Who is your favorite character? Circle One:

     Sabrina   Katie   Randy

     Allison   Stacy   Other

4) Who is your least favorite character?

_____

5) What do you want to read about in Girl Talk?

_____

_____

Send completed form to :
Western Publishing Company, Inc.
1220 Mound Avenue, Mail Station #85
Racine, Wisconsin 53404